DOES THE WORLD NEED AFRICA?

Is Africa a basket case or breadabasket?

Yemi Adesina

CONTENTS

4

APOLOGIA

There are bound to be — only a few, I hope — errors and omissions, and I apologise in advance. No man knows it all, especially me! And you learn more as you get older. One good thing that comes with age is that you are happy to confess when you don't know and pass the inquiry on to a specialist who probably does.

This book is dedicated to hardworking, patient, enthusiastic, generally under-rewarded, and underappreciated people of Africa, those at home and in the diaspora and everyone interested in the welfare of the continent of Africa.

"Let us all remember the destiny of all black people, no matter where they are in the world, is bound up with Africa. We should never forget that famous admonition of the celebrated Jamaican reggae star Peter Crotch when he said, and I quote, "I don't care where you come from, as long as you are a black man, you are an African."

And the lesson for me is our destinies as black people are intricately linked to each other. And we're talking about those on the continent of Africa and the Africans in the diaspora. The urgent responsibility we face is to make our countries and continent attractive for our people to see Africa as a place of opportunity. We must work to help change the African narrative, which has been characterised mainly by a concentration of disease, hunger, poverty, and illegal mass migration.

We must help make Africa a place for investment, progress and prosperity. We have run out of excuses for the state of our continent. We have the manpower, and we should have the political will. It is time to make Africa work. We have good reason to be proud of who we are in the beautiful continent that is ours with its vibrant conscience. Let us make our continent the prosperous and joyful place it should be, and respect will follow."

—Speech by His Excellency The president of Ghana Nana Akufo-Addo December 2022.

"The drums of Africa still beat in my heart. They will not let me rest while there is a single Negro boy or girl without a chance to prove his worth."

—Mary McLeod Bethune. 1875 - 1955)

"Disgust with injustice may sharpen the desire for justice. Readers who don't see this connection merely wish to be entertained, and I have neither skill nor desire to turn the agony of a people into entertainment."

—Ayi Kwei Armah

Foreword

For centuries, Africa was perceived as a continent of poverty, war, and despair. The historical portrayal of Africa as a "basket case" has significantly impacted the continent's economic and social development. Investors and businesses have been hesitant to invest in the continent due to the perception that it is too risky or unstable, leading to poor economic development and a lack of job opportunities, exacerbating poverty and inequality.

However, new perspectives on the continent are emerging as the world becomes increasingly interconnected. Today, Africa is a complex and dynamic continent with a rich history and a bright future. In this book, we proved that 'Africa is a Breadbasket for the World', and explored the many facets of Africa, from its history, rich cultural heritage, and vast natural resources and politics.

You will discover the untapped potential of Africa! But it's not just about business. Africa is home to some of the most beautiful landscapes, wildlife, vibrant arts and music scene. The continent has a wealth of talent, creativity, and potential just waiting to be unlocked.

By investing in Africa, you'll be investing in a continent on the rise and in the future of the world. From innovative startups to thriving industries, the opportunities are endless. Don't miss out on the chance to be a part of Africa's growth and success. So, does the world need Africa? Absolutely!

The Author

Mr Yemi Adesina is the founder of Boyd Agro-Allied Ltd, one of the largest pig farms in Nigeria. He is also the CEO of Pristine Integrated Farm Resources Ltd, a non-profit organisation registered in Africa to promote youth and rural empowerment, alleviate poverty in Africa through education, and improve the productivity and livelihood of farmers.

Mr Yemi, a member of the African diaspora, emigrated to the United Kingdom in 1991. He studied and worked for 20 years and earned his Master's in Business Administration and Master's degree in Social Work in the United Kingdom. In 2010, he emigrated to Africa to contribute to Nigeria's food production.

He is a seasoned farmer and a prolific trainer. He is regularly interviewed on National Television for his outstanding services and achievements within the farming industry and his knowledge of Black African History. He is also a regular writer and contributor to the International PigSite website.

His book, *Profitable Pig Farming: A Step-by-Step Guide to Commercial Pig Farming from an African Perspective,* has become a must and a Blue Bible for those venturing into pig farming in Africa.

He is also the author of *Why Africa Cannot Feed Itself and the Way Forward.* The book considers all factors causing the food crisis and food insufficiencies in Africa, such as geographical variables, climate change, and historical factors like slavery and colonialism. Biological factors, demographic and economic factors, poor leadership and political failures, and weak institutions are also discussed. The book concludes with the way forward for Africa to become food sufficient and a bread basket for the world.

In his book, *What the Ancient African Knew*, he highlights some of the achievements of ancient black Africans and how their works influenced modern life. He looks at the ancient civilisation of Egypt, the first recorded monarch in human history, the continuing internal evolution of Africa's states, and the development of African kingdoms and empires. He proves that the ancient people of Africa had great men and women who accomplished great feats and significantly contributed to world civilisation. This book has helped many young black people around the world feel confident and reassured that, contrary to popular opinion, they are descendants of people from ancient, rich, elaborate cultures that created a wealth of technologies.

Mr Yemi posted 150 videos on YouTube (papayemo1) covering the different aspects of pig farming. Over 2.5 million viewers have watched his videos in over 36 countries, making it one of the most-watched pig farming videos on YouTube from an African perspective.

His Two Days Profitable Pig Farming training, which started over seven years ago, has trained more than 1,000 pig farmers in Nigeria, Togo, Cameroon and Ghana and has led to the establishment of 66 other farms across Nigeria and 3 in Ghana.

Acknowledgements

Although one man has written this book, it wouldn't have been possible without the many people who have been so inspirational and whose research and hard work was helpful during the writing of this book.

I am thankful to God Almighty for His grace to research and put my findings into a book.

I also owe much to the many people who have encouraged me to follow my dream. In particular, my late dad, Mr Solomon Olajide Adesina. And to Bola, my wife of 27 years of marriage. I thank her immensely for her undying love, support, and encouragement, which allowed me to travel, research, and practise farming in Africa for many years.

For my two sons, Femi and Seun, whose input as second-generation African diaspora in the United Kingdom makes the book more relevant to younger Africa. I want to thank them for our lengthy chats and the healthy debates that lasted late into the night and early mornings to gather their perspectives on specific topics. I firmly believe their generation and beyond will move Africa further into the future.

Many people influenced me to start learning about Africa. Some of them I have met in person, and some I know through their teaching, lectures, training, research books and journals.

Coming from all walks of life, the variety of sources, expertise and professions assisted me in approaching the issue from different perspectives, adding much value to this book.

My inspirations were Pastor Matthew Ashimolowo, the late Dr Myles Munro, Dr Mensah Otabil, and Bishop Tudor Bismark. These pastors spent a lot of time teaching and believing Africa could improve.

I am greatly indebted to Dr Howard Nicholas, an economist and researcher at Erasmus University Rotterdam, and Jeffrey D. Sachs et al. for their input on the impact of geography. I am further indebted to Lloyd Timberlake for his book called *Africa in Crisis,* to Jared Diamond for *Guns, Germs, and Steel,* Walter Rodney *for How Europe Underdeveloped Africa.* Finally, I thank Yemi Adeyemi, the founder of ThinkAfrica.net.

1. Introduction

For centuries, Africa was perceived as a continent of poverty, war, and despair. Some often portray the continent as a "basket case", a term used worldwide to describe a poor, underdeveloped, and unstable continent. She is often described as a continent with high unemployment, where many live on less than $1.90 daily. A continent where many children do not have access to necessities such as clean water, healthcare and quality education. A continent with high infectious diseases, such as HIV/AIDS, malaria, and Ebola, and high infant and maternal mortality rates. A continent where many countries experience political instability, including civil war, coups, and authoritarian rule. She is described as a place where corruption has undermined the rule of law and has limited infrastructure, poor roads, and limited access to sanitation.

The historical portrayal of Africa as a "basket case" has significantly impacted the continent's economic and social development. This narrative, created by international organizations and policymakers, which the media have reinforced, has focused on Africa's problems, such as poverty, war, and corruption, rather than its potential for growth and progress.

One of the negative consequences of this portrayal is that it has resulted in a lack of investment in Africa. Investors and businesses have been hesitant to invest in the continent due to the perception that it is too risky or unstable. This has resulted in poor economic development and a lack of job opportunities, exacerbating poverty and inequality.

The portrayal of Africa as a "basket case" has also impacted international aid to the continent. Many aid programs have been focused on addressing immediate needs, such as food aid, rather than investing in long-term development projects that could help to lift people out of poverty. Furthermore, the narrative of Africa as a "basket case" can be seen as a justification for foreign countries and multinational corporations to exploit Africa's resources by promoting the idea that the continent cannot develop without outside help.

Furthermore, the portrayal of Africa as a "basket case" has negatively impacted the continent's self-perception and self-esteem. This narrative has reinforced the idea that Africa is inherently flawed and unable to develop independently, leading to a lack of confidence and pride in the continent's history, culture, and people.

Overall, portraying Africa as a "basket case" has affected the continent's economic and social development. It has resulted in a lack of investment, hindered the effectiveness of international aid, and reinforced negative stereotypes about Africa and its people.

However, despite the negative consequences of the historical portrayal of Africa as a "basket case," new perspectives on the continent are emerging as the world becomes increasingly interconnected. Today, Africa is a complex and dynamic continent with a rich history and a bright future. In this book, 'Is Africa a Basket Case or a Breadbasket for the World', I will explore the many facets of Africa, from its history and culture to its economics and politics.

I believe it is inaccurate to view Africa as either "a basket case" or "a bread basket. Africa has 55 countries with unique cultures and people, each with strengths, challenges, and histories. Africa is home to over 1.2 billion people and more than 2,000 languages, histories, and traditions. Home to many vibrant and thriving societies, the continent is culturally and geographically diverse. Viewing Africa as a monolithic entity that needs to be pitied or assisted out of charity is disrespectful. While there are certainly challenges and issues facing many parts of Africa, there are also many successes and positive developments. For example, many African countries have higher economic growth than the continent-wide average. In 2019, Ghana was one of the fastest-growing economies in the world, with 8.79% growth for the year. Other African countries that saw rapid economic growth in 2019 include Rwanda (7.8%), Ethiopia (7.7%) and Cote d'Ivoire (7.4%). These economies grew significantly more than any major Western nation. It is, therefore, essential to recognize and appreciate Africa's diverse experiences and perspectives rather than making blanket statements about the entire continent.

This book considers Africa's rich cultural heritage, including its art, music, literature, and philosophy. It highlights how Africa has contributed to global cultures through literature, music, and fashion and addresses the challenges of globalization and economic development that Africa faces to preserve its cultural heritage.

Through a deep dive into the current data and research, this book will reveal the true potential of Africa as a breadbasket for the world. From its vast natural resources to its rapidly growing population, some people believe that Africa can become a major economic and political player on the global stage in the coming years and that it is "waking up" to its full potential. However, to realise this potential, African countries must address the challenges of improving education and infrastructure, promoting economic development, and addressing issues related to conflict and corruption. Ultimately, Africa's future will also depend on various complex social, economic, and political factors and will be shaped by the actions and decisions of people within the continent and worldwide.

In this book, you will learn about the current state of Africa's economy, including the major industries and growth areas. It highlights the potential for future economic development in agriculture, technology, and resource extraction. It also addresses Africa's challenges in terms of economic development, such as poverty, corruption, and lack of infrastructure.

Furthermore, the book explores the current state of political stability in Africa, including the role of democratic governments and civil society. It highlights how Africa is working to address conflict issues and human rights abuses and addresses the challenges of political stability, such as ethnic and religious divisions, lack of effective governance, and foreign interference.

We hope this book will educate readers about colonialism and imperialism's historical and ongoing impact on Africa and how it has shaped the continent's current state. The role of international organizations and foreign aid in Africa's development are also key concerns, with the challenges and opportunities they bring.

The book concludes by looking at the valuable lessons that the world can learn from this diverse and resilient continent. Africa is the oldest and the second-largest continent in the world. One of the most important lessons that the history of black Africans teaches us about the world's future is the importance of resistance and resilience in facing adversity. This resilience and determination are a testament to the strength of the human spirit and serve as a powerful example of what can be achieved when people refuse to give up in the face of difficulties. In the future, the world must learn to be prepared to face and overcome the unexpected challenges that will arise, such as climate change, war, crises and pandemics.

This book is a call to action for all interested in understanding Africa's true potential. It is a call to see beyond the stereotypes and misconceptions that have long clouded our understanding of this vibrant continent. I will show you the accurate picture of Africa — a continent rich in resources and human talent but also one plagued by poverty and war.

Overall, this book aims to provide a comprehensive and nuanced understanding of Africa and to inspire readers to see the continent in a new light. It is a clarion call to action for the world to recognize and support Africa's potential and contributions to a brighter future for all. It is a must-read for anyone interested in understanding the continent of Africa and its place in the world. It also provides recommendations for how the world can support Africa's development and cultural preservation.

2. Africa's Economic Contributions to the World

Africa has made significant economic contributions to the world throughout history and continues to do so today. This chapter will examine some key ways Africa contributes to the global economy.

2.1. AGRICULTURAL PRODUCTS EXPORTED FROM AFRICA

Africa is rich in a wide variety of natural resources. Africa is also an important producer of many agricultural products, including coffee, cocoa, and tea. These products are essential for the global food market, and many countries rely heavily on African agricultural products to feed their populations. Some examples of cash crops that are exported from Africa include:

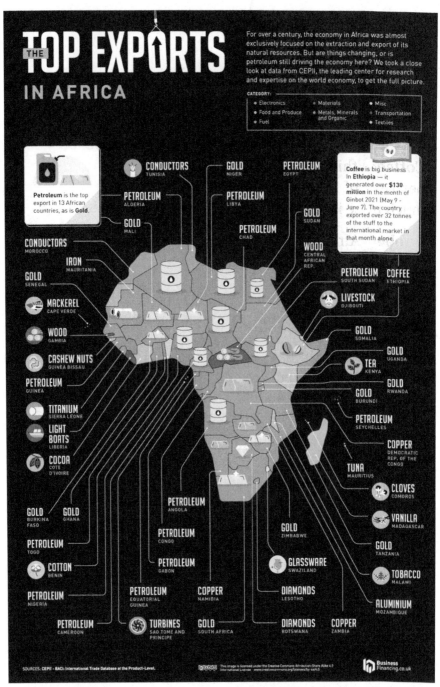

https://vividmaps.com/wp-content/uploads/2021/12/Every-Countrys-Top-Export-and-Import-Map-Africa.png

Cocoa: Africa accounts for 70 per cent of the global cocoa exports Countries such as Ghana, Côte d'Ivoire, and Cameroon are the most significant producers of Cocoa in Africa

Tea: Africa accounts for over 20 per cent of global tea exports. Countries such as Kenya, Malawi, and Rwanda are the most significant producers of Tea in Africa

Coffee: Ethiopia, Uganda, and Tanzania account for about 12 per cent of the world's production, and coffee connoisseurs much prize its beans.

Rubber: Africa accounts for over 14 per cent of global rubber tea exports. Countries such as Ghana and the Ivory Coast are major producers of rubber, which is used in the production of tires and other products

Sugar: Africa is a major sugar producer, accounting for 7 per cent, with the top producing countries including Egypt, Mauritius, and South Africa. Sugar is used in a wide range of food and beverage products.

Cotton: Burkina Faso, Benin, and Mali are major cotton producers, producing 4 per cent of global cotton exports.

Tobacco: Africa is a major producer of tobacco, with significant exports from countries such as Malawi, Zambia, and Zimbabwe.

Fruits and vegetables: Africa accounts for 12 per cent of fruits and vegetables exported globally. Africa exports a wide range of fruits and vegetables, including avocados, pineapples, mangoes, and tomatoes.

Nuts: Africa is a major producer of nuts, including almonds, cashews, and pistachios, with significant exports from Côte d'Ivoire, Morocco, South Africa, and Tanzania. Between 2000

and 2018, world trade in raw cashew nuts was 2.1 billion kilograms, and African producers accounted for almost 66 per cent.

Spices: Africa is also a major producer of spices, including ginger, chilli peppers, and turmeric, with significant exports from countries such as Ethiopia, Ghana, and Madagascar.

Timber and other forestry products: Africa is also a major source of timber and other forestry products used in construction and furniture production.

Other crops: Africa also exports a wide range of other crops, including corn, soybeans, peanuts, sesame, and a variety of fruits and vegetables

Water: Africa has about 9% of the world's freshwater resources. Africa is also home to many of the world's most important water resources, including the Nile, Congo, and Niger rivers, which are vital for agriculture, industry and human consumption.

These resources are important for the global economy, but often, Africa has not reaped the benefits of its resources due to a lack of appropriate policies, corruption, and lack of infrastructure and technology. Many African countries also face challenges in sustainably managing these resources for future generations.

2.2. NATURAL RESOURCES EXPORTED FROM AFRICA

Africa is believed to contain a significant percentage of the earth's remaining minerals. African mineral reserves rank first or second for bauxite, cobalt, diamonds, phosphate rocks, platinum-group metals (PGM), vermiculite and zirconium. The continent also holds significant reserves of rare earth elements used in a wide range of high-tech applications.

NATURAL RESOURCES
World mineral production

Africa produces 5.5% of minerals produced globally **worth $406bn.**

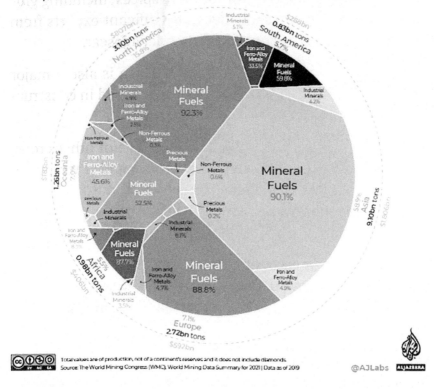

Total values are of production, not a continent's reserves and it does not include diamonds.
Source: The World Mining Congress (WMC), World Mining Data Summary for 2021 | Data as of 2019

@AJLabs

Source: USCS on Aljazeera .com

According to estimates, the continent is home to around 30% of the world's mineral reserves, including 40% of gold reserves, 60% of cobalt reserves, 69% of platinum, 7% of bauxite, 5% of aluminium, 38% of chromite, 9% of copper, 20% of gold, 2% of iron ore, 38% of manganese, 56% of diamond, 8% of petroleum, and 18% of uranium.

However, it is worth noting that not all of Africa's mineral resources have been fully explored, and the estimates may change as further explorations are completed. Some countries may have more abundant resources, and the percentage of the earth's remaining minerals in Africa may vary.

Mining is an important sector for many African countries, but it also poses significant challenges such as environmental degradation, social disruption, and corruption. The mining sector needs to be managed responsibly to ensure that it benefits the local communities, and the countries, while minimizing negative impacts.

Some of the most important minerals found in Africa include:

Oil: Africa is a major oil exporter accounting for more than 9 million barrels per day, about 10% of world output. The top oil-producing countries in Africa include Algeria, Angola, Libya, and Nigeria.

Diamonds: Africa accounts for 62% of the world's diamond production, with countries such as Angola, Botswana, and the Democratic Republic of Congo exporting the gemstone.

Gold: Africa is the world's second-largest producer of gold. The continent accounts for 23 per cent of the global gold production, about 680.3 metric tons per annum, with South Africa, Ghana, and Tanzania being major producers.

Bauxite: Africa is a major producer of bauxite, 30 per cent f the global production. The raw material used to produce aluminium, and Guinea, Ghana, and Mozambique are among Africa's top producers of bauxite.

Copper: Africa is a major producer of copper, with countries such as Zambia, the Democratic Republic of Congo, and Botswana being among the world's top producers.

https://africa.baobab.news/2019/08/05/trading-places-largest-exports-by-country/

Trading places : Largest exports by country

Iron ore: Africa is home to large iron ore deposits, about 4 per cent of global production, with countries such as South Africa, Morocco, and Egypt being major producers.

Uranium: Africa is a major producer of uranium, about 20 per cent of global production,and with countries such as Niger, Namibia, and South Africa being major producers .

Coal: Africa is a major coal producer and is home to some of the world's largest coal reserves, including in South Africa, Mozambique, and Tanzania.

Other minerals: Africa is also a major producer of other minerals, including manganese, phosphate, and tin.

2.3. AFRICAN MINERALS IN YOUR MOBILE PHONE

Most of the electronics we use today are made from minerals extracted from African soil — including aluminium and zinc. In 2021, around 1.5 billion smartphones were sold worldwide — and nearly four in five (78 per cent) people own a smartphone.

More than half of a mobile phone's components — including its electronics, display, battery and speakers — are made from mined and semi-processed materials.

Lithium and cobalt are some of the key metals used to produce batteries. In 2019, about 63 per cent of the world's cobalt production came from the Democratic Republic of the Congo.

Tantalum, extracted from coltan, is used to manufacture tantalum capacitors for portable telephones, personal computers, automotive electronics, and cameras. The DRC and Rwanda are the world's largest producers of tantalum. Together they produce half of the world's tantalum.

Children mining cobalt in Africa   A child playing with a mobile phone in the UK

Coltan mining has financed serious conflicts in the Democratic Republic of Congo, including the Ituri conflict and the Second

Congo War. Coltan is used to make the rechargeable batteries found in cell phones, laptops, electric vehicles, aircraft and power tools. The metal is predominately mined in the Democratic Republic of Congo (DRC), where critics say children as young as seven-years-old labour in horrendous conditions, as shown by the picture above.

African child labour provided labour at a price Europeans could afford, in numbers they required and all to profitable economic use. Thus, Africans were reduced from humanity to inanimate objects of trade and economic calculation. Children's labour was the 'human lubricant' of the whole system.

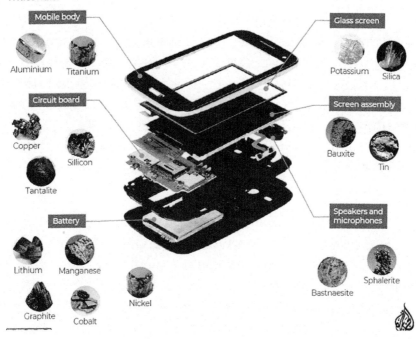

A world of minerals in your mobile phone

More than half of a mobile phone's components - including its electronics, display, battery and speakers - are made from mined and semi-processed. materials.

Mobile body — Aluminium, Titanium

Glass screen — Potassium, Silica

Circuit board — Copper, Sillicon, Tantalite

Screen assembly — Bauxite, Tin

Battery — Lithium, Manganese, Graphite, Cobalt, Nickel

Speakers and microphones — Bastnaesite, Sphalerite

Source: USCS on Aljazeera .com

To sum up, Africa contributes significantly to the world economy through mining, agriculture, manufacturing and human resources. However, it is disappointing that even in this 21st century, Africa is still raped of her resourcesby African leadership and greedy western countries.

2.4. ARE AFRICAN NATURAL RESOURCES A BURDEN OR A BLESSING?

Africa is rich in natural resources, including oil, minerals, and timber. However, despite this wealth of resources, many African countries have struggled with poverty and inequality and their economies have been highly vulnerable to fluctuations in global prices. This phenomenon is known as the "natural resource curse," which has significantly impacted Africa's economic development.

The "natural resource curse" refers to the phenomenon where countries rich in natural resources such as oil, minerals, and timber often experience slower economic growth and development than countries without these resources. Africa is rich in natural resources, and many countries heavily depend on them for their exports and government revenue. This dependence can lead to several adverse effects, known as the natural resource curse.

One of the key effects of the natural resource curse in Africa is a lack of diversification in the economy. Many countries are heavily dependent on a single commodity for their exports, leaving them vulnerable to fluctuations in global prices. This dependency can lead to "Dutch disease" in which the country's other sectors, such as agriculture and manufacturing, suffer due to the overvaluation of the currency due to the high prices of the natural resource exports.

The revenue generated from natural resources is often a significant source of government revenue. If managed improperly, this can lead to corruption, mismanagement of public resources, a lack of government accountability, poor economic development, and human rights abuses.

The natural resource curse sometimes leads to a lack of investment in other sectors such as education, healthcare, and infrastructure. This can negatively impact economic growth and development due to a lack of human capital and basic services.

Additionally, the natural resource curse can also cause conflicts over resources. This can occur when disputes over who has the right to control and benefit from the resources escalate into civil wars and human rights abuses.

One example of Africa's natural resource curse is in Nigeria. Nigeria is the largest oil-producing country in Africa and has been heavily dependent on oil exports for its government revenue and economic growth. However, despite being rich in natural resources, Nigeria has struggled with poverty and inequality, and its economy has been highly vulnerable to fluctuations in global oil prices.

One of the main reasons for this is a lack of economic diversification. The Nigerian economy has been heavily dependent on oil exports, leaving it vulnerable to fluctuations in global prices. This has caused a lack of investment in other sectors, such as agriculture and manufacturing. Additionally, the overvaluation of the currency due to the high prices of oil exports has led to the decline of other sectors.

Another issue is poor governance and corruption. The revenue generated from oil exports has been a significant source of government revenue, but it has not been appropriately managed, leading to corruption and mismanagement of public resources. This has led to poor economic development and a lack of accountability and transparency in using these resources.

Furthermore, the oil industry in Nigeria has also been associated with environmental degradation and human rights abuses. The oil spills and gas flaring have harmed the environment and the local communities, and the government has not addressed these adequately.

Whether Africa is a burden or a blessing is complex and depends on the perspective from which it is viewed. Some argue that Africa is a burden on the world due to its perceived lack of development, political instability, and ongoing conflicts. Others argue that Africa is a blessing, with its abundant natural resources, young and rapidly growing population, and potential for economic growth and development.

 It can be argued that the continent's perceived lack of development and economic underperformance burden the global economy. Africa's low GDP per capita, high poverty rates, and lack of infrastructure are reasons why the continent is sometimes perceived as a burden on the world. Additionally, political instability and ongoing conflicts in some African countries can lead to mass displacement, human rights abuses, and a lack of security. The global media has reinforced this perception, often portraying Africa negatively and perpetuating stereotypes of the continent as a place of war, famine, and disease.

However, this perception of Africa's natural resources being a burden is not entirely accurate or fair. The continent has made significant progress in economic growth, political stability, and human development in recent years. Many African countries have experienced strong economic growth, and there are now more than a dozen African countries that are classified as middle-income countries.

However, the challenges of limited access to markets, credit, and land, as well as lack of infrastructure and technology, have hindered development and made it difficult for these countries to increase their productivity and income.

It is also important to acknowledge that Africa has been negatively impacted by historical and ongoing injustices such as colonization, slavery, and exploitation of resources. The world should address these issues and work towards a more just and equitable relationship with Africa.

In conclusion, whether African natural resources are a burden or a blessing is complex and depends on the perspective from which it is viewed. Africa is a continent with enormous potential, but it also faces significant challenges.

2.5. AFRICA AS AN IMPORTING CONTINENT

While Africa is rich in natural resources, the continent also imports many goods and materials to meet its needs. Africa is a net importer of goods and services, with most of its imports coming from Europe, Asia, and North America.

Africa imports a wide range of goods, including manufactured goods, machinery, vehicles, and chemicals. It also imports food products, such as wheat, rice, meat, fuel, and other energy products.

One of the main reasons for Africa's heavy reliance on imports is the lack of industrialization and economic development in many African countries. Many African countries lack the infrastructure, technology, and skilled labour force to produce goods and materials domestically, making them dependent on imports. Africa's weak institutions and governance, lack of access to markets, and inadequate infrastructure impede the continent's ability to trade, leading to difficulties in exporting and importing goods.

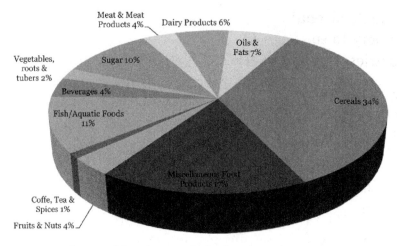

Total West African imports in food products in percentage.
Source researchgate.net (2016).

The import dependency of Africa is a concern because it limits the continent's economic growth and makes it more vulnerable to external economic shocks. Furthermore, the high import dependency also challenges the balance of trade of African countries, as the value of imports often exceeds the value of exports, leading to trade deficits and a negative impact on the countries economies. This affects the exchange rate and makes it harder for countries to pay for their imports, making them more vulnerable to debt and financial crises.

In addition, importing goods can also hurt the local economy by reducing the demand for locally produced goods and services, leading to job losses and a decline in economic activity. This can also discourage the development of local industries, making the country more dependent on imports in the long term while helping to develop other countries.

Some examples of imports to Africa include:

Consumer goods: Africa imports many consumer goods, including clothing, electronics, and household goods.

Industrial equipment: Many African countries import machinery to support their manufacturing and construction industries.

Agricultural products: Some African countries import agricultural products, such as wheat, rice, and other grains, to supplement their own domestic production.

Medical supplies: Africa imports a wide range of medical supplies, including pharmaceuticals, to support the healthcare systems of many countries.

Energy: Some African countries import energy sources, such as oil and natural gas, to meet their domestic energy needs.

Industrial machinery and equipment: Many African countries import industrial machinery and equipment, such as tractors, construction equipment, and manufacturing machinery.

Food products: Africa also imports a significant amount of food, including wheat, rice, and other grains, as well as processed foods.

Fuel: Many African countries import fuel, such as oil and natural gas, to meet their energy needs.

Vehicles and transportation equipment: Africa also imports various vehicles and transportation equipment, such as cars, trucks, and aeroplanes.

2.6. OTHER AFRICAN CONTRIBUTIONS TO THE WORLD

The western economy needs Africa in the same way it needs other regions or countries. The global economy is complex and interconnected; different countries and regions have different roles and functions.

Africa can potentially make significant contributions to the world in the future. The world needs Africa for its economic, cultural, and political contributions and the unique perspective it brings to global issues. Therefore, the global community must support Africa's development and build stronger and more equitable partnerships with the continent. By working together, the world can help Africa fully realize its potential and contribute to a more prosperous and just world.

Africa's key contributions to the world include:

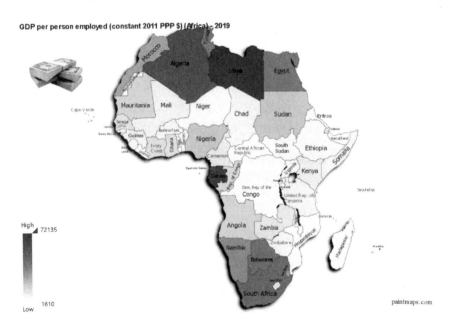

Source: Paintmap.com

Africa is enormous: Africa is the second largest continent in the world. With a total land mass of around 30.3 million Km2, Africa has a population of 1.3 billion people, over 17% of the world population.

Human capital: With a young and growing population, Africa has the potential to become a major driver of the global economy. With 60% of the population under 25, Africa is the youngest continent. This demographic represents a unique opportunity to capitalize on Africa's human capital and build a sustainable future for its people. Like many people worldwide, Africa's young population is creative, connected and dynamic. If African countries can create inclusive economies and provide opportunities for their young people, the continent will become even more important on the world stage.

Market potential: Africa is becoming more reliant on imports, with many countries importing various products, including manufactured goods, technology, and machinery. This trend was facilitated by increasing trade and investment between Africa and the rest of the world. Africa is also home to a large and growing consumer market with over 1.3 billion people. This presents an opportunity for western companies to sell their products and services on the continent.

Global economic interdependence: The interconnectedness of the global economy increasingly means that the economic activities of one country or region can impact the economies of many other countries. Africa is an important part of this global economic interdependence and plays a significant role in the global economy. For this reason, it is in the interest of the western world to ensure that Africa's economy is healthy and thriving.

Climate change solutions: Africa has a unique set of challenges regarding sustainable development, with issues such as poverty, lack of access to basic services, and environmental degradation. Africa has a large proportion of arid and semi-arid land, and many of its communities are already facing the impacts of climate change. The continent can be a leader in sustainable development by developing and implementing innovative solutions that can promote economic growth, protect the environment, improve the quality of living, reduce emissions, and utilize its potential to develop and deploy new technologies.

Innovation and technology: Africa is home to a growing number of entrepreneurs and start-ups, and there are many opportunities for innovation and technology development in areas such as renewable energy, mobile banking, and healthcare. These innovations have the potential to drive economic growth, improve quality of life, and have a positive impact on the global community.

Migration: Africa is a continent of origin, transit and destination for many migrants. In the future, Africa has the potential to play a key role in addressing global migration challenges by developing policies and programs that promote safe and orderly migration and support the integration of migrants into host communities.

Africa has an amazing history and culture: The history of the people and civilizations of the African continent is incredible. The huge range of historical achievements, developments and events have had a lasting impact on the world. Across the continent of Africa, there are 145 UNESCO world heritage sites. This is a testament to the rich history of the people of Africa and shows how important the continent's history is.

Some of the amazing historical sites across Africa include the Pyramids in Egypt, Fort Jeses in Mombasa, Kenya, the Royal Palaces of Abomey in Benin, and the Ruins of Loropéni in Burkina Faso. The ancient city of Timbuktu in Mali has fascinated people for centuries.

All nations in Africa have incredible histories. Although sadly, African history is not as well-known worldwide, the depth and richness of Africa's past is a major reason the continent is important to the world.

Africa also has a rich and diverse culture that inspires people worldwide. Africa's art, music, literature, and other forms of expression have been and will continue to be an important source of inspiration for people worldwide. For example, Nollywood films from Nigeria find audiences around the world. Music from South Africa inspired Paul Simon's Grammy award-winning multi-platinum album Graceland. African fashion and contemporary arts inspire creativity on cat-walks and in galleries from New York to Hong Kong

Africa has amazing wildlife: Africa is important in preserving, protecting and showcasing some of the most fantastic creatures on the planet. With 1,100 species of mammals and over 2,600 species of birds, Africa is one of the most diverse natural habitats in the world. The continent is globally significant as the home of such a huge range of unique creatures.

Many of the animals that live across Africa are famous around the world. Giraffes, zebras, antelopes and hippopotami can only be found in Africa. Countries in Africa are also home to the 'big five' mammals, including lions, leopards, rhinoceros, elephants, and buffalo.

African savannah animals

Many travel from across the world to see Africa's animals. African nations also play a vital role in wildlife conservation, protecting species and ensuring these fantastic animals are around for future generations.

Africa is hugely diverse — Across the 54 African countries, there are more than 2,000 spoken languages. A huge range of religions, including Islam, Christianity, and traditional African religions still practised today. Africa is also important for its natural diversity. From the largest desert in the world — the Sahara, to jungles, savannahs, mountains, lakes and rivers, Africa's landscapes are some of the most varied and impressive in the world.

If there is one thing true about Africa, it's that the continent is among the most varied and diverse places in the world.

Knowledge and research: Africa has a wealth of knowledge and research potential in various fields, such as medicine, agriculture, and renewable energy. The continent has many universities and research institutions working on ground-breaking research and development projects. By investing in research and development, Africa can leverage its knowledge and expertise to contribute significantly to the global community regarding new technologies, improved agricultural practices, and innovative healthcare solutions.

Diaspora engagement: Africa has a large diaspora community worldwide with significant skills, resources and networks. By engaging with its diaspora, Africa can tap into this valuable resource and harness the potential of its citizens abroad to contribute to the continent's development and enhance its global impact. The diaspora can also play a key role in promoting the continent's image, culture and economic opportunities.

Infrastructure development: Africa's extensive infrastructure deficit has hindered its economic growth and development. However, Africa's infrastructure represents a significant opportunity for the continent to attract investment and create jobs. With the right policies and investments, Africa can improve its infrastructure by building new roads, airports, ports, and power plants, thereby enhancing trade and connectivity and spurring economic growth.

Digitalization: Africa has a rapidly growing mobile phone and internet penetration, which is driving a digital revolution on the continent. The digitalization of Africa has the potential to improve people's daily lives, create new opportunities and support sustainable development. From online banking to e-commerce, digital technologies open up new opportunities for Africa to connect with the global economy. Access to information also provides new opportunities for citizens to become more engaged in their own development.

Progress in governance and human development: While narratives over the past few decades have painted a wide range of views of Africa—as a child in need of development, a rising economic power, an imminent threat, a tinderbox of terrorism, as filled with poverty, forced migration, and disease—the truth is, as always, more nuanced. One thing is certain: Africa's transformation in recent decades has been remarkable. Africa is shaping its own destiny and should be referred to as the "African opportunity" instead of the "African threat". By recognizing Africa as an opportunity rather than a threat, governments, citizens, and organizations on the continent and around the world will be better positioned to face current challenges and further boost positive trends.

Across Africa, governance has improved considerably since 2000. Thirty-four countries, home to 72 per cent of Africa's citizens, have improved their governance performance over the last 10 years.

Unfortunately, some elections are still marred by corruption and fraud, and improvements in governance dimensions have not reached all countries. However, as citizens get more educated, they are also becoming more vocal and more equipped to hold their elected officials accountable to the needs of the people.

Responding to conflicts and crises — The African Union has designated 2019 as the "Year of Refugees, Returnees, and Internally Displaced Persons in Africa." This consensus on the importance of African-led solutions to forced displacement indicates the continent's initiative to construct a sustainable solution to migration issues. African countries still host the largest number of refugees globally; Uganda, Ethiopia, and Kenya collectively host about 2.8 million refugees. Despite having few resources, their governments have responded quickly and efficiently to the influx of refugees from neigh-bouring countries.

Improving health and wellness: Africa is facing several health crises, such as the burden of infectious diseases, mater-nal and child health issues, and mental health problems. De-spite these challenges, Africa has made significant progress in addressing these issues and has the potential to be a leader in addressing global health crises. Over the past several decades, significant public health improvements have been made in Africa. There have been substantial declines in maternal and child deaths, and the incidence of chronic malnutrition among children under five has decreased by almost ten per cent from 1995. Most countries are making good progress on preventable childhood illnesses and infectious diseases. HIV/AIDS and ma-laria continue to have a widespread impact on Africans, but treatment options are improving. Across the continent, life ex-pectancies and healthy life expectancies are rising.

To view Africa solely as a hotbed of disease and hunger is to ignore the significant strides that countries and communities have made. African governments and health workers are com-mitted to preventing illnesses, improving treatment access, and finding better ways to deliver quality health care.

Overcoming social challenges: The share of people living in extreme poverty in Africa has declined over the past decades, and, for most countries, the outlook for poverty reduction is positive. Ethiopia, for example, is projected to almost elimi-nate extreme poverty by 2050. However, the concentration of poverty—40 per cent of Africa's extremely poor are projected to live in Nigeria and the Democratic Republic of Congo by 2040—means that the next challenge will be reducing poverty in all countries.

Improvement of non-monetary dimensions of poverty: Many countries, including some of Africa's poorest, are on track to make significant progress on the United Nation's Sustainable Development Goals (SDGs) by 2030. Since 2000, the number of African children enrolled in primary school has increased from 60 million to 150 million. Adult literacy rates are up by almost ten per cent from 1995, and the gender gap in literacy is shrinking, partially driven by massive improvements in gender parity in school enrolment. However, this gender parity needs to shrink further, especially in the sciences, if African countries are to make further economic, political, and social gains.

Improving gender equality: For example, in 11 African countries, women hold almost one-third of parliament seats, more than in Europe and the United States. Women, citizens of democratic countries, and workers receive greater autonomy and power throughout Africa because leaders have started recognising the need for inclusive participation.

2.7. AFRICA AS A SOURCE OF FRESHWATER RESERVE

The potential of an African water resource megahub extends far beyond the continent, with significant implications for the rest of the world. A megahub is a centralized hub for managing, distributing, and utilising water resources across a large region or continent. In the case of Africa, a water resource megahub could have a profound impact on global water security, food security, and energy production.

Researchers from the British Geological Survey and University College London (UCL) concluded that a huge water resource exists in Africa, known as the "African Water Resource Megahub." This vast underground aquifer system is believed to hold over 100 billion cubic meters of water, making it one of the largest known water resources on the continent. The aquifer is located primarily in the northern and central regions of Africa and spans several countries, including Algeria, Chad, Egypt, Libya, and Sudan. The water in this aquifer is primarily from precipitation that fell on the region thousands of years ago and has been stored in porous rock formations. This water resource has the potential to provide a reliable source of water for irrigation, domestic use, and industrial purposes. It could play a crucial role in helping to alleviate water shortages and improve the lives of millions of people in Africa.

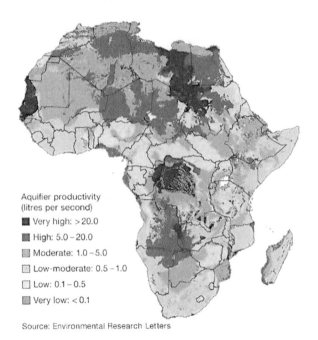

Aquifer productivity
(litres per second)
■ Very high: > 20.0
■ High: 5.0 – 20.0
▨ Moderate: 1.0 – 5.0
▨ Low-moderate: 0.5 – 1.0
☐ Low: 0.1 – 0.5
▨ Very low: < 0.1

Source: Environmental Research Letters

This means that the notoriously dry continent of Africa is sitting on a vast groundwater reservoir. The total volume of water in aquifers underground is 100 times the amount found on the surface. This is contrary to the fact that more than 300 million people across Africa do not have access to safe drinking water. Freshwater rivers and lakes are subject to seasonal floods and droughts that can limit their availability for people and agriculture. At present, only 5% of arable land is irrigated.

However, despite its potential, several challenges must be addressed to utilize this water resourcefully. One of the main challenges is the lack of infrastructure and investment in the region, which makes it difficult to access and transport the water to where it is needed. Additionally, the aquifer is not evenly distributed, and some areas may have more water than others, which could lead to competition and potential conflict over access.

Despite these challenges, there is a growing interest in utilizing this water resource to support sustainable development in Africa. Efforts are being made to increase investment in infrastructure and technology to extract, treat, and distribute water and develop policies and regulations to manage its use.

Overall, the African Water Resource Megahub holds a huge potential for Africa's water security and economic development. It will require a comprehensive and holistic approach involving the cooperation of the international community, local governments and the private sector to realize its full potential.

2.8. THE WORLD NEEDS AFRICA'S HELP TO TACKLE CLIMATE CHANGE

Climate change is a global problem that requires a global solution; every country has a role to play in addressing this issue. However, Africa is set to become increasingly influential in shaping global energy trends over the next two decades as it undergoes the most extensive process of urbanisation the world has ever seen, according to a new report from the International Energy Agency.

Africa's 54 countries produce 2% to 3% of global carbon emissions and are only responsible for 1% of all historic carbon emissions. However, Africa's geographic location makes it set to experience the worst effects of climate change, and five of the most affected countries by recent extreme weather events were African.

Furthermore, the number of people living in Africa's cities is expected to expand by 600 million over the next two decades, much higher than the increase experienced by China's cities during the country's 20-year economic and energy boom. Africa's overall population is set to exceed 2 billion before 2040, accounting for half of the global increase. These profound changes will drive the continent's economic growth, infrastructure development and, in turn, energy demand, projected to rise 60% to around 1,320 million tonnes of oil equivalent in 2040, based on current policies and plans.

Africa has a unique opportunity to pursue a much less carbon-intensive development path than many other parts of the world. To achieve this, it needs to take advantage of the huge potential of solar, wind, hydropower, natural gas and energy efficiency that could lead to a renewable energy revolution. For example, Africa has the richest solar resources on the planet but has installed only 5 gigawatts of solar photovoltaics (PV), which is less than 1% of global capacity.

Africa's natural resources aren't limited to sunshine and other energy sources. It also possesses major reserves of minerals such as cobalt and platinum that are needed in fast-growing clean energy industries.

The continent is rich in natural resources such as solar, wind, and hydropower and has the potential to become a major producer of clean energy. By investing in renewable energy, Africa would not only reduce its own greenhouse gas emissions but also export clean energy to other countries, helping to reduce global emissions.

Gabon has positioned itself as "Africa's green superpower" by using the Congo Basin rainforest — the "lungs of Africa" — as a source for global firms seeking carbon offsets and carbon credits. The Democratic Republic of the Congo, which contains half of Africa's forests, began leveraging the extensive Congo Basin Forest against developed nations through a "pay by performance" scheme to ensure its protection. The project aimed to raise $1 billion to fund a "green development programme" to encourage economic alternatives to logging and farming that have been a traditional income source and the main method through which Indonesian and Brazilian forests have slowly disappeared. The Amazon rainforest, once one of the world's largest and most important carbon sinks, now produces more CO2 than it removes.

Another way Africa can contribute to the fight against climate change is by protecting and preserving its natural ecosystems. The continent is home to a diverse range of ecosystems, from tropical forests to savannah grasslands, and these ecosystems play a critical role in regulating the global climate. By protecting and preserving these ecosystems, Africa can help to maintain the natural carbon sinks that help to remove carbon dioxide from the atmosphere.

Africa can also help to address climate change by promoting sustainable development and economic growth. By investing in sustainable infrastructure, such as public transportation and energy-efficient buildings, Africa can reduce its greenhouse gas emissions while also promoting economic development. Much of the continent is a renewable energy "greenfield" — meaning that some regions can leapfrog directly into embracing renewable energy for a sustainable future without shifting from coal to diesel to gas to nuclear. Just as Nigeria was able to leapfrog fixed-line telephones and directly embrace the power and ability of cell phones, much of Africa can do the same with renewable energy.

In addition to these efforts, Africa can also play a critical role in the global dialogue on climate change. As a bloc, Africa has a unique perspective on the impacts of climate change and can bring valuable insights to the table in international negotiations.

In conclusion, the world needs Africa's help to tackle climate change. The continent has the potential to make a significant contribution through the development and deployment of renewable energy, the protection and preservation of natural ecosystems, and the promotion of sustainable development and economic growth. Furthermore, Africa can be a valuable partner in the global dialogue on climate change, bringing unique perspectives and insights to the table. The international community must provide the necessary support and resources to help Africa take the necessary actions to address climate change. Only through a global effort can we hope to effectively tackle this pressing issue and ensure a sustainable future for all.

3. Africa's Cultural Contributions to the World

In this chapter, we will explore Africa's rich cultural heritage and global impact, demonstrating that Africa's cultural contributions are vital to our understanding of the world's cultural heritage. By examining the various cultural contributions that Africa has made to the world, it will become clear that Africa is a continent that should be celebrated and acknowledged for its contributions to the global cultural landscape.

African history is important to the modern world for several reasons. First, it helps us understand the origins and development of humanity, as Africa is considered the cradle of civilization. Second, African history sheds light on the continent's rich native heritage and its contributions to the world. Third, it provides insight into the political, economic, and social issues that continue to shape Africa and its relations with the rest of the world. Fourth, African history also provides important lessons on colonialism, slavery, and resistance that are still relevant today. Finally, it is important to understand the current global context, as Africa is becoming an increasingly important player in the global economy and international relations.

3.1. ANCIENT AFRICAN CONTRIBUTION TO HUMAN MIGRATION

Ancient Africa played a significant role in human migration, as the continent is believed to be the birthplace of humankind.

The study of human evolution and migration has shown that the first modern humans (Homo sapiens) evolved in Africa around 200,000 years ago and then migrated out of the continent around 100,000 years ago. These migrations eventually led to modern humans' colonization of the rest of the world.

The "Out of Africa" Theory suggests that modern humans evolved in Africa and then migrated to other parts of the world, replacing other hominid species such as the Neanderthals.

The "Multiple Dispersals" Theory: The "Multiple Dispersals" theory suggests that there were multiple waves of migration out of Africa, with different groups of modern humans spreading out in different directions and at different times.

The "African Eve" Hypothesis: The "African Eve" hypothesis suggests that all modern humans descended from a common female ancestor who lived in Africa around 200,000 years ago.

The dispersal of modern humans out of Africa led to modern humans colonising the rest of the world, eventually developing different cultures, languages, and civilizations.

The Bantu Expansion: One of the most significant ancient human migrations out of Africa was the Bantu Expansion, which occurred around 3,000 years ago. The Bantu people, who spoke a common language called Proto-Bantu, migrated from West Africa to other parts of the continent, spreading their culture, language, and agricultural practices. The Bantu Expansion led to the wide spread of ironworking and the development of complex societies. The Bantu migration eventually led to the Bantu people inhabiting most of sub-Saharan Africa and influencing the cultures of the indigenous people.

Trans-Saharan Trade: Another important ancient human migration out of Africa was the trans-Saharan trade, which linked West Africa to North Africa and the Mediterranean. This trade route was used to transport goods such as gold, salt, and enslaved people, and it helped to connect Africa to the rest of the world. The trans-Saharan trade also led to the spread of culture, religion, and technology between Africa and the Mediterranean world.

The Spread of Islam: Islam was brought to North Africa by Arab traders and conquerors in the 7th century. It then spread throughout West Africa via trade routes and the trans-Saharan trade. Islamic culture and religion profoundly impacted Africa, shaping the development of many West African states and societies.

In conclusion, Ancient Africa played a significant role in human migration, as the continent is believed to be the birthplace of humankind. These migrations profoundly impacted the world and its history, leading to the development of different cultures, languages, and civilizations. The study of human migration is ongoing and there are multiple theories, but all of them point to Africa as the origin of humankind.

3.2. AFRICA'S HISTORICAL CONTRIBUTION TO THE WORLD

Africa has made significant historical contributions to the world in ancient times and recent history. Some examples of Africa's historical contributions include:

Ancient Egypt: The civilization of ancient Egypt, which developed along the Nile River in what is now Egypt and Sudan, made significant contributions to the world in the areas of architecture, mathematics, medicine, and hieroglyphics. The ancient Egyptians are also known for their impressive engineering feats, perhaps most famously for constructing the pyramids.

| Moscow Mathematical Papyrus | The Rhind Mathematical Papyrus. Source: ThinkAfrica |

The Spread of Human Civilization: It is believed that human civilization originated in Africa, with the earliest known human fossils found on the continent. The discovery of these fossils has provided crucial insight into our species' evolution and human civilisation's development.

The Spread of Agriculture: Africa is believed to be one of the cradles of agriculture, with evidence of early agricultural practices dating back to around 5000 BCE. The spread of agriculture from Africa significantly impacted the development of human civilization and the rise of early states and civilizations.

Science and Technology: The ancient Egyptians made important contributions to science and technology, including the development of a sophisticated system of writing (hieroglyphics) and mathematics, the invention of the sundial, and the use of the Nile River for irrigation and crop cultivation. The ancient Nubians also developed an advanced water management system, allowing them to grow crops in a desert environment. In West Africa, the ancient Kingdom of Ghana, which existed between the 8th and 11th centuries, made significant contributions to metallurgy, developing a method to extract iron from iron ore and create iron tools and weapons.

Agriculture: Ancient Africa madesignificant contributions to the field of agriculture. The ancient Egyptians developed a sophisticated irrigation and crop cultivation system and greatly understood crop rotation, soil management, and animal husbandry. The ancient Kingdom of Ethiopia was known for its terrace farming and for its production of crops such as coffee, which is now one of the most widely consumed beverages in the world. The ancient Kingdom of Ghana was known for its advanced agriculture system, including irrigation and cultivation of crops like millet and sorghum.

Animal Husbandry: Ancient Africa has a long tradition of animal husbandry, raising cattle, sheep, goats, and pigs. The ancient Egyptians were known for domesticating the Nile River perch, a staple food in ancient Egypt. The ancient Nubians also had a long tradition of domesticating the dromedary camel, which is now widely used in desert regions.

Architecture: The ancient Egyptians are known for their monumental architecture, and the pyramids are considered some of the greatest engineering feats of all time. They also contributed significantly to art, including sculpture, painting, and pottery. The ancient Nubians also developed a unique style of art and architecture characterized by bright colours, geometric patterns, and stylized human figures. The ancient city of Great Zimbabwe, located in present-day Zimbabwe, is an example of a complex architectural achievement. The city was built using dry-stone construction techniques, and it includes a variety of architectural styles, such as curved walls and decorative elements such as stone birds.

Philosophy and Religion: The ancient African civilizations of the Egyptians, Greeks, and Romans developed sophisticated systems of philosophy and religion. The ancient Egyptians believed in an afterlife and developed a complex system of religious beliefs and practices, including the worship of gods and goddesses, the use of amulets and charms, and the practice of mummification. The ancient Kingdom of Aksum, located in present-day Ethiopia, had a rich tradition of philosophy and religion, which included the worship of a pantheon of gods and goddesses and the use of religious texts written in the Geez language.

Medicine and Health: Ancient Egyptians made significant contributions to medicine and health. They developed a sophisticated system of medicine that included the use of herbs and other natural remedies, surgical techniques, and the development of the first known surgical instrument, the surgical needle. They also had a detailed understanding of human anatomy and were able to perform complex surgical procedures such as brain surgery. The ancient Egyptians also developed a comprehensive system of public health, which included the construction of public bathhouses and the development of a system of quarantine to prevent the spread of disease.

Astronomy: The ancient Egyptians also made significant contributions to astronomy. They developed a sophisticated time-keeping system, including sundials and water clocks, and they accurately predicted the Nile River's annual flooding. They also developed a detailed understanding of the stars and planets, which they used for religious and agricultural purposes.

Writing: Ancient Egyptians developed one of the earliest forms of writing, hieroglyphics, which was used for religious texts, legal documents and for recording everyday life. The ancient kingdom of Aksum in Ethiopia also had a writing system called Geez. The Nok civilization of West Africa also had an advanced system of writing that was used to record information about trade, agriculture, and other aspects of daily life.

The arts: Africa has a rich art tradition, including sculpture, pottery, textiles, and jewellery. African art has been an important source of inspiration for artists worldwide, and it has played a significant role in the development of modern art. African art and artefacts are widely collected and exhibited in museums and galleries worldwide.

The spread of language: Africa is home to a diverse array of languages, and many of these languages have been spread around the world through trade, migration, and colonization. African languages such as Swahili and Hausa have become important languages of trade and commerce in many parts of the world, and African words and phrases have been adopted into the languages of many cultures around the world.

Textile: Ancient Egypt, Nubia and Ethiopia were known for their skill in textile production, and they produced various textiles such as linen, cotton, and silk using advanced spinning and weaving techniques. These textiles were highly prized and traded throughout the ancient world.

Mathematics: Ancient Egyptians developed a complex system of mathematics, which included the use of fractions, geometry, and the concept of the unit fraction. They also developed a numeration system using hieroglyphs that could represent both numbers and fractions. The ancient kingdom of Aksum in Ethiopia also had a sophisticated mathematics system, which included a base-60 numbering system similar to the one used in ancient Mesopotamia and the Indus Valley civilization.

Navigation and Seafaring: Ancient Egyptians and Phoenicians were known for their seafaring skills, they developed advanced ships and navigation techniques that allowed them to navigate the Nile River and the Mediterranean sea with ease. This allowed them to trade and establish trade routes with other civilizations. The ancient kingdom of Punt, located in the Horn of Africa, was also known for its seafaring skills and for its trade in exotic goods such as myrrh and frankincense.

The Spread of Ironworking: Africa was one of the first regions in the world to develop ironworking, with evidence of iron smelting in West Africa dating back to around the 3rd century BCE. This technology spread from Africa to other parts of the world, leading to significant advances in agriculture, warfare, and other areas of human activity. The ancient Egyptians were known for their ability to extract and work with metals such as gold, silver, and copper. The ancient Kingdom of Ghana, which existed between the 8th and 11th centuries, made significant contributions to metallurgy, as they were able to extract iron from iron ore and create iron tools and weapons. The ancient Kingdom of Meroe, located in present-day Sudan, was known for its iron-working technology, which included using iron smelting and producing iron tools and weapons.

Music and Dance: Ancient Africa had a rich music and dance tradition. The ancient Egyptians had a complex system of musical notation and a wide variety of musical instruments. The Nubians also had a rich tradition of music and dance that was an integral part of their religious and social life. The ancient Kingdom of Ghana was known for its rich music and dance tradition, which was used to celebrate important events such as weddings and coronations.

The Transatlantic Slave Trade: The transatlantic slave trade lasted from the 16th to the 19th century and profoundly impacted Africa's history. Millions of Africans were forcibly taken from their homes and transported across the Atlantic to work as slaves in the Americas. The slave trade significantly impacted the demographic, economic, and political development of Africa and the Americas.

The Abolition of Slavery: Africa played a significant role in the abolition of the transatlantic slave trade and slavery. Many African leaders and organizations fought against the slave trade and played a key role in the campaign to abolish these practices.

The Scramble for Africa: The Scramble for Africa, the period of colonization and conquest of Africa by European powers that took place between 1884 and 1914, had a profound impact on the continent's history, shaping its political boundaries, economic systems, and cultures.

Pan-Africanism: The Pan-Africanist movement, which emerged in the late 19th and early 20th centuries, aimed to promote the solidarity and cooperation of people of African descent worldwide. It played a key role in decolonization and shaped the continent's political identity.

The Civil Rights Movement: The civil rights movement in the United States and the anti-apartheid movement in South Africa were both heavily influenced by Pan-Africanist ideas and the writings of African leaders such as W.E.B Dubois, Martin Luther King Jr., and Nelson Mandela. Their ideas and activism helped to shape the course of these movements and the fight for racial equality in the United States and South Africa.

The African Union: The African Union, established in 2002, is a continental organization that aims to promote peace, security, and development in Africa. It has played a key role in resolving conflicts and promoting peace.

These are just a few examples of Africa's historical contributions to the world. It is important to note that both positive and negative historical events have shaped Africa's global contributions. The continent's history is complex and multifaceted, and it is essential to consider the different perspectives and historical contexts when studying Africa's contributions to the world.

In conclusion, Africa's contributions to world civilization are wide-ranging and have played a significant role in shaping the course of human history and the development of modern society. From ancient Egypt and the spread of agriculture, iron-working, religion, philosophy, art, language, and technology, to the transatlantic slave trade, the abolition of slavery, the civil rights movement, and the African Union, Africa's contributions to the world continue to shape the present and the future. It's important to acknowledge and celebrate Africa's contributions and recognize that Africa's story is vital to our understanding of global human history.

By recognizing and studying Africa's contributions, we gain a deeper understanding of the interconnectedness of humanity and how different cultures and civilizations have influenced one another.

Furthermore, by understanding Africa's contributions, we can gain a greater appreciation for the diversity of human experience and the richness of human culture, helping to correct stereotypes and misconceptions that often surround the continent of Africa and its people. By acknowledging Africa's contributions, we can also gain a deeper understanding of the root causes of poverty and political instability and develop more effective solutions to these problems.

3.3. ART AND LITERATURE OF AFRICA

Art and literature are important elements of Africa's cultural heritage and have significantly shaped the continent's history and identity.

Art: Africa has a rich art tradition, including sculpture, pottery, textiles, and jewellery. African art is known for its vibrant colours, strong geometric patterns, and symbolic imagery. Traditional African art often reflects the culture, beliefs, and values of the community or group that created it. African art has been an important source of inspiration for artists worldwide, and it has played a significant role in the development of modern art. African art and artefacts are widely collected and exhibited in museums and galleries worldwide.

African art has been an important source of inspiration for artists worldwide. African art, with its use of vibrant colours, strong geometric patterns, and symbolic imagery, has influenced the development of modern art and has been a significant influence on the development of the cubism and abstract expressionism movements. African art has also influenced the development of fashion, textiles, and interior design.

Literature: Africa has a rich tradition of literature, including oral literature, such as folktales, proverbs, and songs, as well as written literature, such as poetry, novels, and plays. African literature reflects the diverse cultures and experiences of the continent's people and deals with themes of love, war, politics, and the human condition. African literature has been widely recognized and celebrated, and many African writers have won international literary awards, such as the Nobel Prize in Literature awarded to Wole Soyinka

Both positive and negative historical events have shaped African art and literature. Centuries of trade, migration, colonization, and globalization feature prominently in African art and literature. As a result, they reflect the complex and multifaceted nature of Africa's history and culture.

African art and literature represent the continent's rich cultural heritage, providing a window into African people's diverse experiences and perspectives. By studying and appreciating Africa's art and literature, we can gain a deeper understanding of the continent's history and culture and how Africa has influenced and been influenced by the rest of the world.

African literature has significantly impacted world literature, bringing new perspectives, themes and styles. They have tackled issues such as race, colonialism, and postcolonialism and helped redefine the boundaries of "world literature." African literature has also influenced the development of film, music, and theatre.

Oral Literature: African oral literature, such as folktales, proverbs, and songs, has had a significant impact on the world. These oral traditions have been passed down through generations and have been a source of inspiration for many cultures worldwide. They have influenced the development of literature and storytelling in many cultures and are an important source of inspiration for modern writers and storytellers.

Music: African rhythms, melodies, and harmonies have influenced the development of jazz, blues, rock and roll, and other genres of music. This impact of African musicians has helped to popularize African music worldwide.

Overall, theart and literature of Africa continue to shape how we see the world. They have influenced the development of music, film, and other forms of expression and continue to inspire new generations of artists and writers around the world. African art and literature have also helped to challenge stereotypes and misconceptions about Africa and its people, and it has helped to promote a greater understanding and appreciation of Africa's cultures and societies.

African Film: African film has changed the face of the global film industry through:

Representation: African film has played an important role in representing Africa's diverse cultures, experiences, and perspectives. African films have tackled many themes, such as love, war, politics, and the human condition.

Aesthetics: African filmmakers have developed a unique visual style incorporating traditional African art and storytelling elements. They have also incorporated elements of African music, dance, and other forms of expression into their films.

Social and Political Commentary: African films have played an important role in addressing the continent's social and political issues. Many African films have tackled poverty, corruption, war, and human rights issues and have helped raise awareness of these issues worldwide.

Festival and Awards: African films have been widely recognized and celebrated at international film festivals worldwide. Many African films have won prestigious awards, such as the Palme d'Or at the Cannes Film Festival and the Golden Bear at the Berlin International Film Festival. This has helped bring greater attention to African film and promote African filmmakers and their work.

Distribution and Consumption: African films have been distributed and consumed around the world. This has helped promote African films and filmmakers globally by increasing their visibility and recognition, breaking down barriers, and exposing the world to diverse stories, perspectives and narratives.

In conclusion, African art, literature and film have had a significant global impact and continue to shape how we see the world. They have influenced the development of film aesthetics, addressed social and political issues, and are widely recognized and celebrated at international film festivals. African film has helped to challenge stereotypes and misconceptions about Africa and its people.

3.4. PRESERVATION AND PROMOTION OF AFRICAN CULTURAL HERITAGE

Preservation: . Preserving African cultural heritage is important to ensure that the continent's rich cultural heritage is not lost. This includes preserving traditional artefacts, such as sculptures, pottery, textiles, and jewellery, and traditional knowledge and practices, such as oral literature, music, and dance. It also includes preserving historic sites and monuments

Promotion: Promoting African cultural heritage is important this can be done through exhibitions, festivals, and other events that showcase African art, literature, music, and other forms of expression. It can also be done through educational programs, books, lectures, workshops, and research projects.

Education: Education is also important for preserving African cultural heritage. This includes educating the public about the importance of preservation and also educating future generations about Africa's heritage and history.

Digitalization: With modern technology, cultural heritage can be preserved through digitalization. Traditional artefacts, such as sculptures, pottery, textiles, and jewellery, can be digitalized through photos and 3D imaging. Traditional knowledge and practices, such as oral literature, music, and dance, are digitalized in written records and video. Historic sites and monuments can be photographed, videoed, and documented for future generations

In conclusion, preserving and promoting African cultural heritage is crucial to ensure that the continent's rich cultural heritage is not lost and to help promote a greater understanding and appreciation of Africa's cultures and societies. This can be done through preservation, promotion, education, digitalization, and partnerships.

3.5. MISCONCEPTIONS AND STEREOTYPES ABOUT AFRICA

Africa has long been plagued by misconceptions and stereotypes that have distorted our understanding of the continent. These stereotypes about Africa are inaccurate and harmful but remain pervasive in media and pop culture. They have obscured Africa's complexity and diversity and led to a lack of understanding and appreciation for its true potential.

Despite Africa's many challenges, the vast continent is faring better than many imagine. Studies have shown that when it comes to Africa, public perception of countries often lags behind reality. This lag is attributed to its colonial history, and the media seem better at capturing fast-moving crises and catastrophes in Africa than slow-moving improvements. For example, only 4.1% (172,000) of the 4.3 million COVID-19 deaths reported globally are in Africa. From a continent with a population of 1.2 billion and poor health care, Africa's COVID statistics can be compared to the United States which has significantly better medical facilities, yet their deaths counted for 11% (500,000) of global deaths. Even though this comparatively low mortality from COVID-19 numbers significantly defies early predictions of a mass COVID-19 catastrophe, there is still minimal publicity about this from the media. This kind of media misconception about Africa is similar to what China received in the early 2000s when many continued to think of China as poor and backward.

This section aims to challenge these stereotypes and provide a more nuanced and accurate understanding of Africa.

Some of the most common misconceptions and stereotypes include:

Africa is a Homogeneous Continent: One of the most pervasive stereotypes is that Africa is a monolithic entity, with all its countries and peoples being the same. This stereotype ignores the vast cultural, linguistic, and political diversity that exists within Africa. Africa has 55 countries with unique cultures, home to over 1.2 billion people, and more than 2,000 languages, histories, and traditions. Africa is also a huge continent, covering more than 30 million square kilometres, and it is home to many landscapes, including deserts, rainforests, mountains, and savannahs. This stereotype ignores that Africa is a continent of rich cultural, linguistic, and natural diversity.

Africa is Poor and Underdeveloped: Africa is often portrayed as poor and underdeveloped, with images of poverty, hunger, and disease as the most common images associated with the continent. This stereotype ignores that Africa is a continent of economic growth and potential, with many countries experiencing rapid development and urbanization. Many African countries are experiencing strong economic growth and attracting foreign investment. Last year, six of the world's fastest-growing economies — Ghana, Ivory Coast, Senegal, Djibouti, Ethiopia and Tanzania — were African. Many African countries are experiencing the growth of a middle class with a growing number of innovative and entrepreneurial individuals and businesses to cater for their needs and want. The SMEs are slowly and consistently driving economic growth and development and a growing consumer market with increasing demand for a wide range of goods and services

Africa is Plagued by War and Conflict: Africa is often portrayed as rife with civil war, genocide, and ethnic conflict. While it is true that poverty and war are serious problems in many parts of Africa, this stereotype ignores the many successes and achievements of the continent. Africa is home to some of the fastest-growing economies in the world, and many countries are making significant progress in reducing poverty and promoting peace and stability. Life expectancy has also improved. A newborn baby in Africa today has an average lifespan of 65 years. This is a far cry from a few decades ago when the crises of Aids, malaria and tuberculosis had cut life expectancy to below 50 in several African countries.

Africa is a Continent of "Primitive" People: This stereotype is associated with the idea that Africa is a "backward" continent whose inhabitants are "primitive" and in need of "civilizing." Africa is perceived as full of natural resources but lacking in human capital. This stereotype is not only racist but also completely ignores the fact that Africa is home to a large and rapidly growing population with a youthful and highly educated workforce. With the right policies and investments, Africa's human capital has the potential to drive economic growth and development.

A Place of Constant Crisis and in Need of Rescue: Africa is perceived as a continent inherently plagued by corruption, poor governance, and a lack of the rule of law. A continent where corruption is endemic and governments are ineffective, leading to poor economic performance and a lack of development. This stereotype is limiting and harmful, as it perpetuates the idea that Africa cannot solve its problems. This representation can discourage investment, trade, and tourism and ignore that Africa has a rich history and culture and is full of resilient, entrepreneurial and innovative people. This stereotype also ignores that corruption is a global problem and that many African countries have significantly improved governance and reduced corruption.

Africa is a Continent that is not Open to Change: This stereotype perpetuates the belief that traditional customs and practices are still dominant and Africa is not open to change. This stereotype is particularly pervasive regarding issues such as women's rights and LGBT rights, with the assumption that Africa is inherently conservative and resistant to change. This stereotype is untrue and undermines the fact that many African countries are making progress in these areas. Africa is even ahead in some areas of improving gender equality. For example, in 11 African countries, women hold almost one-third of parliament seats, more than in Europe and the United States.

A Continent of Disease and Poor Health: While it is true that many parts of Africa face significant health challenges, such as high rates of malaria and HIV/AIDS, this stereotype ignores the many successes and advancements in healthcare on the continent. African countries are making significant progress in expanding access to healthcare, improving maternal and child health and tackling infectious diseases. Over the past several decades, there have been substantial declines in maternal and child deaths, and the incidence of chronic malnutrition among children under five has decreased by almost ten per cent from 1995. Most countries are making good progress on preventable childhood illnesses and infectious diseases. HIV/AIDS and malaria continue to have a widespread detrimental impact on Africans, but treatment options are improving. Across the continent, life expectancies and healthy life expectancies are rising.

A Continent that lack of Infrastructure and Poor Governance. While these are certainly challenges in many parts of the continent, many African countries have made significant strides in improving infrastructure, governance, and institutions. Africa has made progress by building roads, ports, airports, and telecommunications, which are fundamental for economic growth and development.

In conclusion, the misconceptions and stereotypes about Africa can be limiting and harmful and undermine the continent's potential contributions to the global economy. They obscure the true complexity and diversity of the continent and limit our understanding of Africa's rich cultural heritage, economic potential, and contributions to the global community. This book aims to challenge these stereotypes and misconceptions and provide a more nuanced and accurate understanding of Africa, its people, cultures, challenges, and opportunities.

4. The State of Africa's Economy

The state of Africa's economy is characterized by a mix of both positive and negative developments. On the negative side, the continent is plagued with economic challenges such as poverty, inequality, and lack of access to essential services. However, Africa has recently made significant economic progress, and many countries are experiencing strong growth in various sectors.

Africa has been growing steadily in terms of Gross Domestics Product (GDP) growth, with an average growth rate of around 3-4% in the last decade. However, some countries have performed better, such as Ghana, Ethiopia and Senegal, while others have performed worse, such as Angola.

Regarding GDP per capita, Africa is still a relatively poor continent, with an average GDP per capita of around $1,500. Some countries have performed better, including South Africa, Gabon, and Mauritius, while others have performed worse, such as Burundi and Malawi.

One of the most notable areas of progress has been agriculture. Many African countries have invested in irrigation, mechanization, and other technologies to boost agricultural productivity and diversify their crops, which has led to improved food security and increased exports. For example, Ethiopia has seen significant growth in its coffee and flower exports, while Ghana has become a major cocoa producer. This has increased in-

comes for farmers and rural communities and has helped reduce poverty in these areas.

According to a database of new investments maintained by EY
professionals, petroleum and mining industries have accounted for more than half of Foreign Direct Investment (FDI) in the
past seven years. The trend is even more pronounced in the
46 jurisdictions of sub-Saharan Africa. Manufacturing is also
thriving, particularly in countries with a strong manufacturing
base, such as Egypt and South Africa.

Africa has made significant progress in telecommunications.
Mobile phones are one of the most powerful drivers for economic growth in Africa — the number of mobile-phone subscribers
surged by 2,500% from 2000 to 2019, with many countries now
having near-universal access to mobile phones. This increase in
connectivity and access to information has positively impacted the continent's economy as Africans use mobile phones for
commerce and communication, creating a new value chain. The
e-commerce industry is also growing rapidly. The first and most
famous example of telecommunications creating a value chain
is M-Pesa, the Kenyan mobile-money platform. It was created
to send money between people and has blossomed into a mar-
ketplace. Kenyans can use it to buy insurance, pay a barber, bor-
row money, or finance a pay-as-you-go solar power system.

South Africa has the most developed sub-Saharan economies
and its deepest capital markets. South African retailers are
among the most visible brands across the continent, such as
MTN, the telecommunications provider, and Shoprite, the su-
permarket chain.

Another area of growth in Africa's economy is the tourism
sector. Africa has a wealth of natural and cultural attractions,
from wildlife safaris in East Africa to the beaches of West Af-

rica, from the ancient pyramids of Egypt to the Victoria falls in Zambia. The tourism sector has the potential to generate significant economic benefits, including job creation, foreign exchange earnings, and the development of infrastructure. However, tourism was affected by the COVID-19 pandemic, with many countries closing their borders and imposing travel restrictions. Recently, countries are opening their borders again, and tourism is on the rise.

Another key area in which Africa has made progress is developing infrastructure. Many countries on the continent have invested in building roads, railways, and ports, which has improved transportation and made it easier for businesses to operate. Additionally, there has been significant progress in expanding access to electricity, with many countries increasing the number of people with access to power. This investment evolution reflects the improvement in governance and stability that began in the 1990s. Democratic institutions are established and recognized, and fewer people live in extreme poverty. However, these democratic transitions remain fresh and fragile, with countries progressing at different speeds. These investments are expected to positively impact the continent's economic growth and development, enabling the movement of goods and services, reducing transportation costs, and improving the overall business environment.

The Renewable energy sector is another area of growth in Africa's economy. Africa has abundant renewable energy resources, such as solar, wind, and hydropower, and many countries are now investing in developing these resources to meet their growing energy needs. Renewable energy is also essential for reducing poverty and promoting economic growth, and it can provide access to electricity in rural areas and benefit business development and industry.

Many countries on the continent are investing in technology and innovation, which has the potential to drive economic growth and development. For example, there has been an increase in tech startups and incubators helping to create jobs and promote innovation.

A growing middle class is another sign of progress in Africa's economy. As incomes have risen, more people can afford to purchase goods and services, driving economic growth and development. Additionally, a growing middle class has helped to create a more stable and sustainable economy, as they tend to be more invested in the long-term development of their countries.

Finally, the financial sector is another critical area of growth in Africa's economy. Many countries are working to improve the overall business environment and promote economic growth by developing their financial sectors. This includes the development of banking systems, the creation of financial regulatory frameworks, and the establishment of stock markets. Regarding international trade and investment, Africa is becoming integrated into the global economy, with many countries signing trade agreements and attracting foreign investment. This is helping to drive economic growth and development, but governments also need to ensure that trade and investment benefit the local population.

There has also been progressing in reducing poverty and promoting economic inclusion. Many countries have implemented policies and programs to improve poor and marginalised communities access to healthcare, education, and financial services. This has helped to reduce poverty and improve the standard of living for many people on the continent.

Governance and political stability have also improved. Many countries on the continent have made significant progress in terms of democratization and good governance. This is reflect-ed in the holding of regular and fair elections, the strengthen-ing of institutions, and the protection of human rights. These developments have helped create a more stable and predict-able environment for businesses and investors, contributing to economic growth and development.

Lastly, many countries have been working to increase trade and integration regionally and globally. This has helped to cre-ate a more connected and integrated economy, which can lead to increased economic growth and development.

Long-term trends, measured over decades instead of years, show that African countries are now more attractive invest-ment destinations. Africa is becoming the last region of the world offering a demographic dividend: The median age is 18 for the continent, 14 years younger than any other, and Africa is the only place with its birth rate certain to stay above the replacement rate. For the foreseeable future, Africa will have a growing number of young people as consumers and workers. That makes a move beyond extractive investment that much more critical. Natural resource investments create relative-ly few jobs and even fewer skilled jobs. "Investments in other sectors are needed to create good jobs and address other de-velopment goals."

It is projected that investment rationales will be based on country-level economics and on urban areas, corridors and regions. Leading cities, such as Lagos (Nigeria), Johannesburg (South Africa) and Nairobi (Kenya) will benefit greatly from fi-nancial technology hubs, middle-class consumers and connec-tivity. This is because Africa's leading cities account for 80% of consumers with the disposable income to acquire assets such as cars, televisions and appliances. Other leading cities in sub-Saharan Africa are Luanda, Angola; Khartoum, Sudan; Dar es Salaam, Tanzania; and Addis Ababa, Ethiopia.

Nigeria and Ethiopia are the only countries in sub-Saharan Africa with 100 million people or more. Nigeria is also a known investment destination for oil and gas and hosts an emerging technology hub and start-up culture. Ethiopia is home to Ethiopian Airlines, the continent's largest airline, which makes Addis Ababa an emerging transportation hub.

Ghana and Kenya stand out for their relative political stability and economic diversification. Both export natural resources but aren't dependent on any single one. Their challenge is to develop more domestic supply chains to generate economic value before exporting. Côte d'Ivoire, on Ghana's western border, is another example of diversification. Together, the two countries produce about two-thirds of global cocoa output.

In conclusion, the current state of Africa's economy is characterized by a mix of positive and negative developments, with steady GDP growth and low GDP per capita. Agriculture, extractive resources, and manufacturing are the major industries in Africa, with technology and e-commerce sectors, tourism, infrastructure, renewable energy, and the financial sector emerging as growth areas. The continent is also seeing an increase in foreign investment and trade, which is helping to drive economic growth and development. However, the continent still faces many challenges, including poverty, corruption, and lack of infrastructure. Despite these challenges, many African countries are working to improve the overall business environment and promote economic growth. This includes efforts to improve governance, reduce corruption, and promote entrepreneurship. Many countries are also working to improve education and healthcare and increase access to electricity and other basic services.

4.1. THE POTENTIAL FOR FUTURE ECONOMIC DEVELOPMENT

Africa has significant potential for future economic development in agriculture, technology, resource extraction, climate change and population.

Agriculture: Africa is home to 60% of the world's uncultivated arable land, which means that a significant amount of fertile land currently remains unused for agricultural purposes. This land can be used for growing crops, raising livestock, and other forms of food production, which could help boost food security and economic development. Agriculture has the potential to drive economic growth and development. The continent has a diverse range of climates and vast and fertile lands, and soil types, allowing for various crops. With suitable investments in irrigation, mechanization, and other technology and infrastructure, Africa can become a major exporter of agricultural products and become a significant player in the global food market, boosting food security, creating jobs, improving livelihoods, and reducing poverty. In addition, Africa has a rapidly growing population. With the increasing demand for food, agricultural exports can be a major source of foreign exchange for many African countries. To fully realize the potential of Africa's agriculture, there needs to be a focus on investing in modern technology, infrastructure, and extension services, which can help to increase productivity, competitiveness, and efficiency. This includes access to modern seeds, fertilizers, and irrigation systems, as well as mechanization and precision agriculture technologies to increase yields and reduce the labour needed.

In addition, investing in modern storage and processing facilities is also vital for the potential of agriculture development. Modern facilities can help to reduce post-harvest losses, increase the shelf life of products, and improve the quality of the produce, making them more attractive to buyers and fetching a better price. Another important aspect to consider is the development of value chains and market linkages, particularly in high-value crops such as fruits, vegetables, nuts and spices. Farmers need to be connected to markets to increase their generated income. Furthermore, investing in research and development is crucial to identify the most profitable and sustainable crops and the best ways to grow them.

Climate change is also a significant challenge for Africa's agriculture, and addressing this issue is crucial for the potential of agriculture development. Climate change can be addressed through investing in climate-smart agriculture, water management, and sustainable land use practices to make agriculture more resilient to the impacts of climate change.

Technology: Technology is another key area of potential for future economic development in Africa as it can help to bridge the gap between the continent and the rest of the world. The growing use of technology, such as mobile phones and the internet, has helped connect people and businesses in Africa to the global economy and created new trade and investment opportunities. Additionally, technology can improve the delivery of services in healthcare, education, and financial services, which can aid efforts to reduce poverty and improve the standard of living. Increased access to technology also creates a favourable environment for technology startups, helping to drive innovation and entrepreneurship.

Resource Extraction: Resource extraction is another area of potential for future economic development in Africa, leveraging its natural resources to drive economic growth and development. The continent is rich in natural resources, such as oil, natural gas, and minerals. These resources can be a major source of revenue and foreign exchange for many African countries. With the right policies and regulations in place, resource extraction can be done in a sustainable way, and the benefits can be shared equitably with the local population. Additionally, Africa has a growing renewable energy sector, which can help to address the continent's energy needs and reduce dependence on fossil fuels.

Africa's Large and Growing Population: Africa's large and growing population has the potential to be a significant driver of economic growth and development. The continent has over 1.2 billion people, which is projected to grow in the coming years. A large population can provide a significant source of labour and consumers, and a larger workforce will increase productivity and output, leading to economic growth. Additionally, a larger population can also help to create jobs, particularly in sectors such as manufacturing, agriculture, and services, which can help to reduce poverty and improve living standards.

Africa's large population will also drive economic growth through consumption. A larger population means more consumers, which drives demand for goods and services, particularly in retail and consumer goods. A growing population can also lead to a growing middle class, which benefits the country through a more stable and sustainable economy.

Furthermore, Africa's large and growing population also has the potential to drive innovation and entrepreneurship, as more people can generate more ideas and start new ventures. With increasing internet and digital platforms access, this population will be a major force in the digital economy.

For Africa's population to drive economic growth, proper education and training are necessary to ensure that the workforce is equipped with the skills needed to compete in the global economy. Also, providing basic social services such as health-care and education to the population is crucial.

In conclusion, Africa has significant potential for future economic development in agriculture, technology, and resource extraction. These sectors can drive economic growth and development, create jobs, and improve the standard of living for the continent's people. In addition, Africa's large and growing population has the potential to be a significant driver of economic growth and development. A larger workforce and more consumers can help to increase productivity and output, create jobs, and spur demand for goods and services. With the right policies and investments, Africa's population can be a major force in the global economy.

4.2. EXTERNAL FACTORS DRIVING CHANGE IN AFRICA

Africa is a continent that has experienced a significant change in recent decades, driven by both internal and external factors. Despite widespread poverty and substantial social problems, Africa is doing better than many imagine. Much changed for the continent during the turn of the century, galvanising a period of rapid growth and development.

The Role of International Organizations and Institutions: Organizations such as the African Union, the World Bank, and the International Monetary Fund have significantly shaped the continent's economic and political developments. The African Union, for example, has been instrumental in promoting peace and security, while the World Bank and the IMF have provided financial assistance and advice to many African countries. For example, the Heavily Indebted Poor Country (HIPC) Initiative forgave $100B of multilateral, bilateral and commercial debt in

30 African countries. This assistance allowed them to escape from the burden of endless debt servicing.

The Entry of China into Africa: The entry of China into Africa has been a significant development in the continent's recent history. China has become one of the largest investors in Africa, investing in a wide range of industries, including infrastructure, mining, and energy.

China has invested a significant amount of money into Africa in recent years. According to estimates, China's investment in Africa has grown rapidly, from around $1 billion in 2005 to over $60 billion in 2019. The investments have been in various sectors, including infrastructure, mining, energy, agriculture, real estate and finance. China has also provided loans to African countries, estimated to be around $148 billion as of 2019. It's worth noting that these figures are estimates and the actual amount invested by China in Africa may be higher or lower.

The result was a flurry of construction of roads, ports and airports in a continent crying out for better infrastructure. Although there have been concerns that countries such as Angola and Zambia may be stoking another debt crisis, many Africans argue that China's arrival has been a net benefit to the continent. There are many positives to the Africa-China relationship. The Chinese see opportunities because of demographics and developments that show Africa will play a major role in the world.

In China's wake have come others, including Turkey, India, Brazil and the Gulf States, who have imagined a commercial and strategic opportunity in Africa that their western counterparts have been slower to spot. In population terms, Africa is the continent that will see the most growth over the next decades. By 2050, its population is forecast to more than double to 2 billion. By the end of the century, it will likely double again, when more than one in three people on earth will be African. Although that will pose vast challenges for governments seeking to improve living standards, it does mean that in brute aggregate terms, African markets are likely to grow for decades.

The Global Economy has Significantly Impacted Africa: The increasing demand for African resources, such as oil, minerals, and agricultural products, has led to economic growth in many countries. Foreign aid and investment from developed countries have significantly driven economic and social change in Africa.

Climate Change: Climate change is also a major external factor affecting Africa. The continent is particularly vulnerable to the impacts of climate change, such as droughts, floods, and sea level rise, which can have devastating effects on agriculture and food security.

International Migration is also an external factor that has significantly impacted Africa. Many Africans have migrated to other parts of the world for better economic opportunities, which has led to positive and negative consequences for the continent. On the one hand, the remittances sent back by migrant workers have provided a significant source of income for many families and communities. On the other hand, the loss of skilled workers and entrepreneurs can negatively impact economic growth and development.

The Influence of the Western Media: Western influences have played a role in shaping how Africa is perceived and represented in the global media and contributed to creating stereotypes and misconceptions about the continent.

International Politics and Global Power Dynamics have also influenced African development. The Cold War, for example, had a significant impact on the continent, as many African countries aligned themselves with either the Soviet Union or the United States. The ongoing War on Terror continues to shape many African countries' security and political landscape.

Overall, the external factors driving change in Africa are diverse and complex, and they have had both positive and negative impacts on the continent. Understanding these factors is crucial for understanding Africa's challenges and opportunities and developing effective policies and strategies for addressing them.

4.3. IMPACT OF SLAVERY AND COLONIALISM ON AFRICA'S CURRENT ECONOMY

The transatlantic slave trade and the Scramble for Africa, both during the 18th and 19th centuries, had a profound and lasting impact on the continent's current economy. These historical events shaped Africa's economic development in ways that continue to be felt today.

One of the most significant impacts of slavery and the Scramble for Africa on the continent's economy is the loss of human capital. The transatlantic slave trade resulted in the forced migration of millions of Africans, many of whom were skilled workers, farmers, and artisans. This loss of human capital devastated Africa's economy, resulting in a shortage of skilled labour and a lack of technological and economic development.

Furthermore, the Scramble for Africa led to the exploitation of Africa's natural resources. European powers extracted valuable resources such as gold, diamonds, and rubber, which were then used to fuel the industrialization of Europe. This extraction of resources led to the depletion of Africa's natural resources and the underdevelopment of its industries. Furthermore, the exploitation of resources was done primarily for the benefit of the colonizing powers, and the profits generated from these resources were not invested back into the continent, leading to a lack of economic development.

Slavery and the Scramble for Africa also led to the displacement of traditional economies and the imposition of cash crops, which profoundly impacted the continent's economy. European colonizers forced local communities to grow cash crops such as cotton, coffee, and cocoa, which were then exported to Europe. This led to the disruption of traditional economies, which were based on subsistence agriculture, and the displacement of local communities. This displacement led to the loss of land and livelihoods, further impoverishing the continent.

Additionally, the Scramble for Africa led to the creation of artificial borders. The borders were drawn with little regard for ethnic and cultural boundaries, which led to the fragmentation of ethnic and economic groups. This fragmentation made it difficult for African countries to trade and cooperate, hindering the development of a regional economy.

In addition, slavery and the Scramble for Africa led to the development of a dependency culture, where African economies became heavily dependent on exporting raw materials and importing manufactured goods. This dependency led to a lack of economic diversification and made African economies vulnerable to global market fluctuations.

Furthermore, the transatlantic slave trade and the Scramble for Africa also resulted in cultural heritage and knowledge loss. The forced migration of millions of enslaved Africans resulted in the loss of labour loss, traditional knowledge, customs, and cultural practices.

In conclusion, the transatlantic slave trade and the Scramble for Africa had a profound and lasting impact on Africa's current economy. The loss of human capital, the exploitation of resources, the displacement of traditional economies, the creation of artificial borders, the development of a dependency culture, forced labor and migration, and the imposition of economic structures designed to benefit colonizing powers all contributed to the underdevelopment of the continent. The legacy of slavery and the Scramble for Africa continues to shape the continent's economy. It highlights the need for African countries to take control of their own resources and development in order to create a more sustainable and equitable economy.

4.4. IMPACT OF CORRUPTION ON THE DEVELOPMENT OF THE AFRICAN ECONOMY

"Illicit financial flows are multidimensional and transnational. Like the concept of migration, they have countries of origin and destination and several transit locations. Therefore, the process of mitigating illicit financial flows cuts across several jurisdictions. These jurisdictions may protect fake charitable organizations, facilitate money laundering, warehouse disguised corporations and conceal anonymous trust accounts. Ironically, the fact remains that the funds involved often come from jurisdictions with scarce resources for development financing, depleted foreign reserves, drastic reduction in collectable revenue, tax underpayment or evasion and poor investment in-flows."
—His Excellency Muhammadu Buhari,
President of Nigeria

Corruption is a significant problem in many African countries, and it has far-reaching and devastating impacts on individuals, communities, and the continent. The impact of corruption in Africa can be seen in several areas, including economic development, governance, and the provision of basic services.

One of the most significant impacts of corruption in Africa is on economic development. Corruption has impeded economic growth by distorting markets, creating new business entry barriers, and discouraging foreign investment. Corruption has also led to the misallocation of resources and the diversion of public funds intended for economic development, resulting in wasted resources and a lack of improved living standards.

Corruption also undermines governance in Africa. When corrupt officials are more likely to prioritize their own interests over the interests of the public, this can lead to poor policy decisions and a lack of accountability for public officials, contributing to poor governance. Additionally, corruption erodes public trust in government and creates a culture of cynicism and apathy, making it harder for democratic institutions to function effectively.

Another impact of corruption in Africa is on the provision of basic services. Corruption leads to the diversion of funds intended for public services such as education, health care, and infrastructure. This contributes to existing issues of inadequate services and poor living conditions for citizens. Corruption also creates barriers to accessing basic services, as people may need to pay bribes. This severely impacts the poor and vulnerable, who may not have the resources to pay bribes and may be forced to go without essential services.

In conclusion, corruption is a pervasive problem in many African countries, and it has far-reaching and devastating impacts on individuals, communities, and the continent. The impact of corruption can be seen in areas such as economic development, governance, and basic services. Addressing corruption in Africa is essential for promoting sustainable development and improving the lives of citizens.

Several underlying causes of corruption in Africa include colonisation, weak institutions, lack of accountability, and poverty.

Colonialism has had a significant impact on the development of corruption in Africa. The legacy of colonialism can be seen in many African countries, where the institutions and systems put in place by colonial powers continue to shape the political and economic landscape.

One of the main ways that colonialism has contributed to corruption in Africa is by creating a legacy of weak institutions. During the colonial period, colonial powers often prioritized their own interests over the needs of the local population. This led to the establishment of institutions that were designed to serve the interests of the colonial powers rather than the needs of the local population. This legacy of weak institutions has persisted in many African countries, making it difficult to create strong and effective institutions that can provide oversight and accountability, which can facilitate corruption.

Another way colonialism has contributed to corruption in Africa is by creating a legacy of economic inequality. Colonial powers often exploited African resources and labour for their own gain, contributing to wealth and power imbalances. These imbalances continue to shape the economic landscape in many African countries, where a small elite controls a large portion of the wealth, creating a power imbalance that allows them to influence government decisions and engage in corrupt practices to maintain their wealth and power.

Colonialism also emphasised ethnic and tribal divisions in Africa by imposing arbitrary borders and promoting divide-and-rule policies, which has led to conflict and violence that continues to this day. These divisions facilitate corruption as some groups may take advantage of the conflict to amass wealth and power .

Another cause of corruption in Africa is the weakness of institutions. In many African countries, there is a lack of strong and effective institutions that can provide oversight and accountability. This allows individuals and groups in positions of power to engage in corrupt practices without fear of consequences. Additionally, weak institutions contribute to a lack of transparency, making it easier for corrupt individuals and organizations to conceal their activities.

Another major cause of corruption in Africa is the lack of accountability. In many African countries, there is a lack of effective mechanisms for holding individuals and organizations accountable for their actions. This lack of accountability allows corrupt individuals and groups to operate with impunity and can perpetuate a culture of corruption.

Poverty is also a major cause of corruption in Africa. Many people in Africa live in poverty and may be more likely to engage in corrupt practices to survive. This can include accepting bribes to secure employment or contracts, or embezzling funds intended for public projects. Additionally, poverty can also make people more vulnerable to corruption, as they may be more likely to accept bribes or engage in other corrupt practices to access basic necessities such as food and shelter.

In many African countries, there is a lack of transparency in allocating government resources and awarding contracts. This lack of transparency makes it difficult for citizens to hold their leaders accountable and can facilitate corrupt practices such as embezzlement and nepotism.

Another cause is the cultural acceptance of corruption in some societies. In some cultures, corruption is viewed as a necessary evil or a way of doing business. This cultural acceptance can make it difficult to change attitudes and behaviours related to corruption and make it harder to hold corrupt officials accountable.

The lack of civic engagement and political participation also contributes to corruption. When citizens are disengaged and do not hold their leaders accountable, corrupt officials can operate without fear of repercussions. On the other hand, when citizens are actively engaged and demand transparency and accountability, it can help to deter corruption.

Finally, corruption in Africa is also driven by external factors such as foreign aid and investment. In some cases, foreign aid and investment are directed to corrupt officials or organizations rather than to the intended recipients, perpetuating corruption and undermining development efforts.

In conclusion, corruption in Africa is a multifaceted and complex problem with various causes. These causes include weak institutions, lack of accountability, poverty, lack of transparency, lack of an independent judiciary, high levels of inequality, lack of civic engagement and political participation, lack of effective anti-corruption laws and enforcement, cultural acceptance of corruption, and external factors such as foreign aid and investment. Addressing these underlying causes and implementing effective anti-corruption measures are crucial for reducing corruption in Africa and promoting sustainable development

4.5. THE DRIVERS OF WAR AND CONFLICT IN AFRICA

A complex interplay of political, economic, and social factors causes war and conflict in Africa. Understanding the underlying causes of war and conflict in Africa is essential to find practical solutions.

Political factors are one of Africa's leading causes of war and conflict. Many African countries have a history of ethnic and tribal divisions, which can lead to tensions and conflicts between different groups. Additionally, many African countries have also experienced a lack of democratic governance, which has led to political repression and marginalization of certain groups, creating fertile ground for rebellion and civil war.

Another major cause of war and conflict in Africa is economic factors. Many African countries are rich in natural resources, such as minerals and oil, which can be a source of wealth and power. However, these resources can also be a source of conflict, as different groups may compete to control these resources, leading to war and violence. Additionally, poverty and economic inequality also contribute to conflicts, as people may resort to violence to gain access to resources and improve their economic situation.

Social factors also contribute to war and conflict in Africa. Ethnic and religious divisions can lead to tensions between different groups, escalating into violence over issues such as land disputes and forced displacement.

Finally, external factors can also play a role in war and conflict in Africa. Many African countries have been subject to colonization and foreign intervention, which can lead to political instability and conflicts. External actors provide support and resources to armed groups, which can prolong and escalate conflicts.

Weapons are the lifeblood of any conflict or war. Consequently, the fighting rages on as long as there is a continuous supply of weapons. However, eliminating weapons and conflicts may end, gradually die a natural death, or become significantly less destructive. Harmless non-violent groups advocating for a cause can suddenly become dangerous and destructive when sufficiently equipped with arms.

According to Stockholm International Peace Research Institute (SIPRI), ten countries account for 90% of all global weapons export. And the world's top five significant arms exporters, from highest to lowest, are the United States, Russia, Germany, France, and China. Together, these five nations account for 74% of global weapons exports. The other five are the UK, Spain, Israel, Italy, and the Netherlands. These wealthy nations, directly or indirectly, supply most of the weapons used to fight in Africa. The irony of this is that the five permanent members of the UN Security Council — the Unities States, the United Kingdom, France, China and Russia — are among the top 10 arms dealers, and their weapons are being used to perpetrate violence in Africa and the world.

Africa as a continent has experienced the fastest inflow of arms and weapons than any other region in the world. African governments and rebel groups 2014 imported 45% more weapons, with Algeria, Morocco, and Sudan leading the pack. The arms export industry commands over $400 billion annually.

In conclusion, war and conflict in Africa are caused by a complex interplay of political, economic, social, and external factors. Addressing these underlying causes is essential to find effective solutions to these issues. This can include promoting democratic governance, addressing economic inequality and poverty, promoting social cohesion, and addressing external factors such as foreign intervention.

4.6. THE IMPACT OF POLITICAL INSTABILITY ON AFRICAN ECONOMIC DEVELOPMENT

The current political stability in Africa is a complex and nuanced issue. While some countries have made significant progress in democratic governance and civil society, others struggle with ongoing conflicts, human rights abuses, and authoritarian rule.

In terms of democratic governance, many African countries have made significant progress in recent years. Many countries have transitioned to democratic government systems and have held regular, free, and fair elections. Countries such as Ghana, Senegal, and Namibia are examples of successful democratic transitions. However, there are still countries on the continent where democratic governance is weak or non-existent.

Civil society also plays a significant role in promoting political stability in Africa. Civil society organizations, such as NGOs and advocacy groups, often serve as a voice for marginalized communities and hold governments accountable. In many countries, civil society groups have played a key role in promoting democracy, human rights, and good governance. However, civil society organizations face significant challenges in some countries because of government repression and lack of resources.

However, there are also challenges facing political stability in Africa. Some countries struggle with ongoing conflicts and human rights abuses, which can devastate economic development. Some countries have authoritarian governments that repress civil society and violate human rights, making it difficult for citizens to participate in the political process.

The role of ethnic and religious divisions is an important factor to consider when discussing the current state of political stability in Africa. In some cases, these divisions have led to violent conflicts and have hindered political stability. In other cases, ethnic and religious divisions have been used by political leaders to maintain power and repress opposition groups. Addressing these divisions and promoting unity and reconciliation is crucial for achieving lasting political stability in many African countries.

Another important factor to consider when discussing the current state of political stability in Africa is the international community's role. Many African countries rely on foreign aid and investment to support economic development and promote political stability. However, the actions of international actors can also have a negative impact on political stability. For example, the imposition of sanctions or the withdrawal of aid can lead to economic instability, and foreign military intervention can exacerbate ongoing conflicts. International actors need to work closely with African governments and civil society to promote stability and economic development.

Political instability has a significant impact on economic development in Africa. When countries are plagued by ongoing conflicts, human rights abuses, and authoritarian rule, it is difficult for businesses to operate and for people to participate in the economy. This can lead to economic stagnation and increased poverty.

During conflicts, roads, bridges, and other infrastructure can be destroyed, making transporting goods and services difficult. This causes shortages of essential goods like food and medicine and makes it difficult for businesses to operate. Additionally, the destruction of infrastructure can make it difficult for people to access basic services, such as healthcare and education.

Political instability also leads to mass migration and population displacement, making it difficult for people to participate in the economy. People forced to flee their homes often lose their livelihoods, making it difficult for them to rebuild their lives and lead to increased poverty.

In addition, political instability always leads to the erosion of the rule of law and the weakening of institutions. When political stability is lacking, institutions such as the judiciary and the police can become ineffective, increasing crime and corruption.

In conclusion, political instability can significantly impact African economic development by destroying infrastructure, causing mass migration and population displacement, discouraging foreign investment and trade, weakening institutions and increasing corruption. This makes it difficult for businesses and people to participate in the economy. Addressing political instability is crucial for promoting economic growth and development in Africa.

4.7. THE CHALLENGES OF ECONOMIC DEVELOPMENT

Africa faces several challenges in terms of economic development, such as poverty, corruption, and lack of infrastructure.

Poverty and Inequality: Poverty is one of Africa's most significant challenges in terms of economic development. Despite recent economic growth, poverty remains widespread on the continent, with many people living on less than $1.90 a day. When large portions of the population live in poverty, it leads to social unrest and makes it difficult for governments to maintain stability. Similarly, when wealth and resources are concentrated in the hands of a small elite, it can lead to widespread frustration and mistrust of government institutions. Poverty is a major obstacle to economic growth and development in Africa, as it limits people's ability to access basic services such as healthcare and education, making it difficult for people to participate in the economy.

Lack of Infrastructure is also a major challenge that Africa faces regarding economic development. Many African countries lack basic infrastructure such as roads, ports, airports, and power generation, which makes it difficult for businesses to operate and for people to access basic services. This lack of infrastructure also increases the cost of doing business and makes it difficult for African countries to compete in the global economy.

Weak Institutions: When institutions such as the judiciary, legislature, and civil service are weak or non-existent, it can make it difficult for countries to achieve political stability and economic development. When democratic accountability is lacking, it can lead to authoritarian rule, human rights abuses and lack of transparency, which can also contribute to political instability.

Lack of Skilled Workforce Many African countries have a large youth population but lack the necessary skills and education to participate in the modern economy. This lack of a skilled workforce can make it difficult for businesses to operate and for countries to attract foreign investment. It also limits the potential for economic growth and development, making it difficult for countries to take advantage of new technologies and business opportunities.

Lack of Access to Finance: Many African countries lack access to finance and have underdeveloped financial systems. It becomes difficult for businesses to access the capital they need to grow and create jobs. This lack of finance access can also limit businesses' opportunities to invest in new technologies and expand their operations.

Political Instability and Ongoing Conflicts: Political instability and ongoing conflicts can lead to mass displacement, human rights abuses, and a lack of security, making it difficult for businesses and countries to attract foreign investment. It undermines economic growth and development and often leads to humanitarian crises.

International Cooperation: International cooperation has played a key role in promoting African political stability. The African Union, the United Nations and other international organizations have been working together to promote stability, resolve conflicts and support democratic transitions.

However, it's important to note that the role of international actors in promoting political stability can be a double-edged sword. While international actors can provide valuable support to African countries, their actions can also have negative consequences. Foreign military intervention can exacerbate ongoing conflicts, the imposition of sanctions can lead to economic instability, and corrupt governments can misuse foreign aid. International actors can also perpetuate the lack of political stability in Africa by imposing policies that are not in line with the real needs and capacities of the countries they are trying to help. For example, imposing democratic transitions without considering a country's culture and the root causes of political instability, such as the legacy of colonialism, inequality, poverty, and weak institutions. Without addressing these underlying causes, it will be difficult for international actors to promote lasting stability in Africa.

In conclusion, Africa must address the issues of poverty, corruption, and lack of infrastructure before significant economic development can occur. These interrelated challenges make it difficult for African countries to achieve sustainable economic growth and development. Addressing these challenges will require a comprehensive approach that understands the lasting effects of colonialism and how to strengthen local institutions rather than relying on foreign aid.

5. Prosperous Africa Means a Prosperous World

Can a prosperous Africa mean a prosperous world? This book believes that when Africa achieves its potential and overcomes its challenges, it can contribute to global economic growth, stability, and prosperity.

Economic Growth: Africa has a young and growing population, representing a significant opportunity for the continent to capitalize on its human capital and build a sustainable future for its people. With the right investments in education, healthcare, and other basic services, Africa's young population could become a valuable resource for the global economy and society. This could increase productivity, provide more jobs, and greater economic growth.

Trade and Investment: A prosperous Africa will increase trade and investment between Africa and the rest of the world. As the continent's economies grow, it will become a more attractive destination for foreign investment, which can help to create jobs and boost economic growth. This increased trade and investment can also lead to new markets, benefiting businesses and consumers worldwide.

Innovation and Technology: Africa's potential in innovation and technology can help to drive global economic growth and improve people's lives. The continent's entrepreneurs and startups are developing new technologies to address global challenges such as climate change and poverty, which can benefit the entire world.

Sustainable Development: A prosperous Africa can also contribute to sustainable development globally. By developing and implementing innovative solutions that can promote economic growth, protect the environment, and improve people's lives, Africa can become a leader in sustainable development and an example for other countries to follow.

Peace and Security: A stable and prosperous Africa can contribute to global peace and security. When countries can achieve economic growth and development, it can lead to greater stability and reduce the risk of conflict.

Cultural Exchange: It will also lead to increased cultural exchange between the continent and the rest of the world. As Africa's economy grows, it will become a more attractive destination for tourists and cultural exchange programs, which can lead to a greater understanding and appreciation of African culture. This cultural exchange will foster mutual respect and understanding between different cultures and communities, leading to greater peace and stability.

Humanitarian Aid: A prosperous Africa will also reduce the need for humanitarian aid. Economic growth and development lead to improved living conditions and access to basic healthcare, education, and clean water. This can help to reduce poverty, improve health outcomes, and increase resilience to natural disasters and other emergencies.

Climate Change: A prosperous Africa can contribute to the global fight against climate change. As Africa's economy grows, it can increase its capacity to invest in renewable energy, energy efficiency, and sustainable infrastructure. This can reduce the continent's carbon emissions and help mitigate the impacts of climate change.

Diaspora Engagement: It will lead to increase engagement with its diaspora worldwide. As the continent's economy grows, it can tap into its citizens' skills, resources, and networks abroad, further driving economic growth and development.

Education It will lead to increase access to education for people across the continent. With better economic conditions, more resources can be invested in education, leading to improved literacy rates, better educational outcomes, and more opportunities for people to improve their lives. Access to education is also a large factor in reducing poverty and improving health outcomes.

Health: A prosperous Africa will also lead to improved health outcomes for people across the continent. With better economic conditions, more resources can be invested in healthcare, leading to better access to medical care, improved health outcomes, longer life expectancy, and more opportunities for people to improve their lives.

Gender Equality will also lead to greater gender equality on the continent. With better economic conditions, more resources can be invested in programs that promote gender equality, which can lead to greater opportunities for women and girls and a more equitable society.

Environmental Protection: this will lead to greater environmental protection. With better economic conditions, more resources can be invested in environmental protection, leading to greater conservation efforts and a more sustainable future.

Infrastructure: This will lead to improving infrastructure on the continent. With better economic conditions, more resources can be invested in building and maintaining infrastructure such as roads, airports, ports, and power plants. These improvements will support trade and increase connectivity between cities and countries, spurring economic growth and creating jobs.

Financial Inclusion: It will lead to greater financial inclusion on the continent. With better economic conditions, more resources can be invested in building and improving financial systems, which can lead to more people having access to banking and other financial services.

Human Rights: This will lead to greater respect for human rights on the continent. With better economic conditions, more resources can be invested in ensuring everyone is treated with dignity and respect, regardless of their background. In a more inclusive society, everyone can participate fully in the economic, social, and political life of their communities.

In conclusion, a prosperous Africa means a prosperous world as it contributes to global economic growth, stability, and prosperity. Africa's potential for economic growth, innovation and technology, sustainable development, peace and security, cultural exchange, humanitarian aid, climate change, and diaspora engagement can positively impact the world. The global community needs to support Africa's development and build stronger and more equitable partnerships with the continent to create a just and sustainable future for all.

5.1. THE ROLE OF AFRICA IN THE FUTURE GLOBAL LABOUR MARKET

Studies show that there will be an estimated shortage of 85 million workers around the globe by 2030. Typically, a labour shortage occurs when there are not enough available workers participating in the labour market to meet the demand for employees. For example, there were nearly 11 million job vacancies in the United States in 2022. There were over 1.2 million open job roles in Europe, and Australia had 400,000 vacant positions. This labour shortage is undoubtedly one of the biggest challenges in modern history and could significantly impede the world's ability to fully recover in a post-pandemic market.

Here are some of the factors driving the labour shortage.

1. **COVID-19**: As of March 2022, WHO has reported more than 6 million people deceased due to pandemic-related issues, while millions of others are dealing with the long-term effects of the virus.

2. **Mental Health Issues:** The global pandemic severely impacted workers' mental health. The U.K.'s Office of National Statistics reports that one-half of the over 400,000 employees who left the workforce during COVID did so due to long-term mental health issues.

3. **Migrant Workers Make Up 5% of the Global Workforce**: The pandemic significantly hindered this dependency as countries set stricter immigration policies to control the spread of the virus within their borders. In the U.K., immigration rates fell by 90% in 2020.

4. **Shift in Workers' Expectations**: Throughout the pandemic, many employees faced additional pressures at work, such as sudden layoffs, lockdowns, and extraordinary personal chal-

lenges, including homeschooling their children. A recent study by Monster shows that 95% of workers are open to changing jobs, and 92% are willing to change industries if necessary.

5. **Low Wages**: The ongoing labour shortage has created a candidate-driven market in most areas of the world, and some are leaving for higher salaries.

6. **Aging Population** — Another factor impacting today's labour shortage is the world's ageing population. For instance, in the U.S. alone, 10,000 people per day reach the 65-year-old threshold for retirement. Studies estimate that by 2030, one in six people will be aged 65 or over.

7. **Birth Rates are Falling**: The combination of an ageing population and a falling birth rate means fewer people will be available to work. China's working population will drop by 20%, and Japan's by 40%.

8. **Technology Skills Gap**: According to a recent study, 87% of global employers admit that they are struggling with the loss of skills and experience through retirement.

With its large and growing population, Africa has a significant role in the future global labour market. The continent is projected to have the largest workforce in the world by 2040, with an estimated 1.1 billion working-age people. This presents a vast opportunity for Africa to contribute to the global economy and help alleviate labour shortages in other parts of the world by providing a source of migrant workers. Migration can help fill labour shortages in other parts of the world, particularly in industries that lack skilled workers. Some African countries already have a history of exporting migrant workers and have a reputation for providing a skilled and hard-working labour force.

With so many western countries struggling with production and supply chain challenges, there will be an increased push for migrants of young people from Africa.

Manufacturing experts predicted a global labour shortage of over 8 million workers. Logistics is another sector struggling to attract workers, and the U.K. is seeing a shortage of over 100,000 truck drivers. The healthcare industry in the U.K. had a shortage of 150,000 care workers in 2022. These are gaps that Africa's young workforce can fill and benefit from.

One of the key ways that Africa can contribute to the global labour market is by increasing the education and skills of its workforce. This can help create a larger pool of qualified workers who can fill in-demand roles in various industries. Investing in education, vocational training, and apprenticeship programs is critical to make this happen. By providing these opportunities, Africa can help to produce a highly skilled workforce that can compete in the global market and meet the demand for skilled labour in other parts of the world.

Africa can also contribute to the global labour market by increasing women's participation in the workforce. Women in Africa tend to have lower levels of education and fewer opportunities for paid work than men, which can contribute to labour shortages. However, measures to increase female participation in the workforce will address this imbalance and increase the supply of available workers. Policies that support women's economic empowerment, such as affordable childcare and flexible working arrangements, are necessary to implement this change.

In conclusion, Africa has a significant role in the future global labour market. With a large and growing population, the continent has the potential to provide a highly skilled and diverse workforce that can help to alleviate labour shortages in other parts of the world. By investing in education and skills development, increasing the participation of women in the workforce, and providing a source of migrant workers, Africa can help to contribute to the global economy and play a key role in shaping the future of the global labour market.

5.2. THE ROLE OF AFRICA TO THE WORLD IN THE NEXT 50 YEARS

In the next 50 years, Africa will play a crucial role in shaping the world's future. The continent is home to a rapidly growing population and a wealth of natural resources, making it a key player in the global economy.

Meeting the World's Energy Needs: Africa will also play a crucial role in meeting the world's energy needs in the next 50 years. The continent has vast reserves of oil, natural gas, and other resources that will be needed to power the world's economies. Africa will also be a key player in developing renewable energy sources, such as solar and wind power, which will be essential in sustainably meeting the world's energy needs. This development has already begun in some countries with large-scale projects such as the Lake Turkana Wind Power project in Kenya, which is set to become the largest wind farm in Africa, and the Noor Ouarzazate Complex in Morocco is the world's largest concentrated solar power plant. Africa also has the potential for hydroelectric power, with several large hydroelectric dams already in operation and more under construction. For example, the Grand Ethiopian Renaissance Dam on the Blue Nile is set to become the largest hydroelectric power plant in Africa when completed.

In addition to renewable energy, Africa has significant fossil fuel reserves, particularly oil and natural gas. While fossil fuels have been a major source of revenue for some African countries, the increasing concern over climate change and the need to transition to cleaner energy sources has led to a focus on diversifying Africa's energy mix.

The World's Food Security The continent will also play a vital role in the world's food security, as Africa has vast fertile lands capable of producing various crops. The world's population is projected to reach nearly 10 billion by 2050, and Africa will be an important food source to feed this growing population. The continent is home to various agricultural systems, including rainfed and irrigated cropland, pastoral systems, and agroforestry. These all have the potential to produce a wide range of food crops, including cereals, root crops, fruits, vegetables, and livestock products. Additionally, Africa has a large population of smallholder farmers who are well-suited to take advantage of these opportunities and contribute to increasing food production.

There is also a growing focus on sustainable agriculture in Africa, which aims to increase food production while preserving the environment and protecting natural resources. This includes practices such as agroforestry, conservation agriculture, and integrated pest management, which can help to increase yields and reduce the negative impacts of farming on the environment.

Africa's Demographic and Economic Growth will Shape the World: One of the key drivers of Africa's growth is its demographic trend. The continent has a large and young population, which is projected to continue growing in the coming decades. By 2050, Africa's population is expected to reach 2 billion, and by 2100, it could reach 4 billion. The economic growth in Africa is also likely to have a significant impact on the global economy. As Africa's economies continue to grow and develop, it is expected to become an increasingly important market for goods and services and an important source of labour and human capital. This can lead to increased trade, investment, and economic integration between Africa and other regions of the world and could also lead to the emergence of new global economic powerhouses on the continent. This will create new opportunities for trade and investment and help reduce poverty and promote economic growth.

Africa's Role in the Field of Technology and Innovation: Africa can play a significant role in innovation and technology in the next 50 years. The continent's demographic and economic growth, combined with a growing focus on innovation and technology, suggests that Africa has the potential to become a major player in the global technology landscape.

One of Africa's key drivers of innovation and technology is the rapid growth of the continent's mobile and internet infrastructure. The widespread adoption of mobile phones and the increasing availability of internet access create new opportunities for innovation and technology development. This increased access has led to the emergence of new technologies such as mobile banking, mobile health, and mobile education, which are helping to improve people's lives across the continent.

Another important driver of innovation and technology in Africa is the growing number of young people entering the workforce. Many of these young people are well-educated and have the skills and knowledge necessary to participate in the global economy, which is expected to lead to increased innovation and technology development on the continent.

Poverty: Africa has a large population of people living in poverty, and poverty reduction is a central goal of sustainable development in the continent. The continent's economic growth and development and the expansion of social protection programs will be key to reducing poverty and promoting inclusive economic growth. Additionally, the efforts to promote access to education, healthcare and other essential services, as well as create job opportunities, can also help reduce poverty.

Inequality: Despite progress in reducing poverty, inequality remains a significant issue in many African countries. Income inequality, as well as inequality in access to education, healthcare, and other essential services, is a major challenge in the continent. Addressing inequality will require policies and programs that promote inclusive economic growth and ensure that the benefits of economic growth are shared more widely. This includes progressive taxation, targeted social protection programs, and efforts to increase access to education, healthcare, and other essential services for marginalized groups.

Africa's Role in Global Governance and Decision-Making: Africa is likely to play an increasingly important role in global governance and decision-making in the next 50 years. The continent's demographic and economic growth and its growing political influence suggest that Africa will have a growing voice in shaping the global agenda on a wide range of issues.

One of the key drivers of Africa's growing role in global governance is the continent's demographic trend. Africa has a large and young population, which is projected to continue growing in the coming decades. This growing number of young, educated, and politically active citizens will demand greater global governance representation. As Africa's economies continue to grow and develop, it is expected to become an increasingly important market for goods and services and an important labour and human capital source. This is likely to lead to increased trade, investment, and economic integration between Africa and other regions of the world and could also lead to the emergence of new global economic powerhouses on the continent.

Africa has also been increasing its representation and influence in global governance institutions. The African Union has been working to increase the continent's representation in international organizations such as the United Nations and the World Trade Organization. Africa is also increasingly participating in international climate change and sustainable development negotiations.

Africa's Role in Healthcare and Medicine: Africa can play a significant role in healthcare and medicine in the next 50 years. The continent is facing a number of healthcare challenges, including high rates of infectious diseases, maternal and child mortality, and a shortage of healthcare workers. However, there are also a number of factors that suggest Africa has the potential to make significant progress in addressing these challenges in the coming decades.

Africa's growing population in the coming decades will increase the demand for healthcare services and provide a large pool of potential healthcare workers.

Another important driver of Africa's role in healthcare and medicine is the increasing investment in the healthcare sector. In recent years, there has been increasing investment in healthcare infrastructure and human resources in Africa, which is helping to improve access to healthcare services and increase the number of healthcare workers on the continent. Additionally, there is a growing focus on innovative and sustainable healthcare solutions, such as telemedicine and community health workers, which can help improve access to healthcare services in remote and underprivileged areas.

Africa is also becoming a leader in the research and development of new treatments and vaccines, particularly in tropical medicine and infectious diseases. African countries and institutions are participating in the global effort to discover treatments and vaccines for COVID-19. They have also been involved in researching and developing treatments for other infectious diseases such as Malaria, tuberculosis and HIV/AIDS.

Africa's Role in Tourism: Africa has the potential to play a significant role in the field of tourism in the next 50 years. The continent is home to a diverse array of natural landscapes, wildlife, and cultural heritage sites, which make it an attractive destination for tourists. One of the key opportunities for Africa in tourism is the continent's natural and cultural resources. Africa is home to a wide range of natural landscapes, from the savannas and deserts of the north to the rainforests of the central and southern regions. Africa is also home to a diverse array of wildlife, including iconic species such as lions, elephants, and gorillas, which are a major draw for tourists. Furthermore, Africa's cultural heritage is also an important tourist attraction, with a rich history and cultural diversity found throughout the continent. As tourists become more conscious of their impact on the environment and local communities, there is an increasing demand for sustainable and responsible tourism options. Africa can capitalize on this trend by promoting sustainable tourism practices, such as ecotourism, community-based tourism, and responsible wildlife tourism. Africa's tourism industry has the potential to be a major source of economic growth, as well as to promote cultural exchange and understanding.

In conclusion, Africa will be crucial in shaping the world's future in the next 50 years. The continent's young and growing population, vast natural resources, the potential for economic growth, technological innovation, entrepreneurship, and addressing global challenges, as well as its increasing participation in global governance and decision-making, will significantly impact the world in the next half-century.

5.3. WHAT AFRICA NEEDS TO TAKE ITS POSITION IN THE WORLD

For Africa to achieve these goals and play a significant role in shaping the world's future in the next 50 years, there are several key steps that the continent needs to take.

First, Africa needs to invest in education and training to develop a skilled workforce that can take advantage of the opportunities presented by the growing global economy African government will need to invest in primary, secondary, and tertiary education, as well as in vocational training and apprenticeships.

Second, Africa needs to invest in infrastructure and technology to support economic growth and development. This can be accomplished by investing in transportation infrastructure, such as roads, railways, and ports, as well as in energy infrastructure, such as power plants and transmission lines. Additionally, investing in technology and internet connectivity will promote innovation and entrepreneurship.

Third, Africa needs to develop policies and institutions that promote economic growth and development. It is important to create a conducive business environment for private sector investment, implement policies to promote entrepreneurship and small and medium-sized enterprises and strengthen institutions that promote good governance and the rule of law.

Fourth, Africa needs to address the challenges of poverty and inequality. This includes developing and implementing policies and programs that promote inclusive economic growth, such as targeted social safety nets, and investing in health and education services to ensure that all citizens have access to these basic services.

5.4. CAN AFRICAN COUNTRIES COPY CHINA'S INDUSTRIALISATION EXPERIENCE

The belief in the power of industrialization to drive development is now a mainstay of development agendas by African leaders who are faced with increasingly youthful and often jobless populations and higher accountability to their citizenry. Rising labour costs in China, an ageing population, and political imperatives have led economists to argue that there is an impending relocation of millions of manufacturing jobs from China to developing countries. African countries are positioning themselves as recipients of these manufacturing jobs. They are establishing Special Economic Zones (SEZ) as one way to achieve industrialization and attract Chinese investment.

In the late 1970s and early 1980s, the Chinese government announced an "opening-up strategy" and set up pilot SEZs. For China, a relatively developing country at the time with limited financial resources, clustering industries together in the same location (technical services, repair and maintenance, administrative and legal services, logistical services, packaging, etc.) was crucial and necessary. It created economies of scale and efficiency.

It is often suggested that African countries should look to China as a model for industrialization. However, there are some differences between China and African countries.

The Level of State Control Over the Economy: China has a highly centralized government that can make quick and decisive economic decisions, while many African countries have weak and ineffective governments that struggle to implement effective industrial policies. Additionally, China has a large and relatively well-educated workforce. In contrast, many African countries have high poverty levels and limited access to education, making it difficult to attract and retain skilled labour.

The Infrastructure Development Level: China has invested heavily in infrastructure, including roads, bridges, ports, and power generation, greatly facilitating industrial development. In contrast, many African countries have limited infrastructure, which makes it difficult for businesses to operate and for goods and services to be transported, hindering the growth of industries.

Large Domestic Market: China has a large domestic market which allows companies to access a wide range of consumers and provides a strong incentive for businesses to invest in the country. Africa, due to Balkanisation, has a relatively small domestic market, and many countries lack the necessary economic diversity to sustain industrial growth.

Balance Trade: Before industrialization, China did not have a poor trade balance. The government, while industrializing, took steps to protect the Chinese domestic market for domestic manufacturers, thereby carefully managing imports for non-productive consumption. Most African countries do not have the opportunity to do this — their domestic markets are already highly liberalized, and many have trade deficits with China.

Relaxed Rules Around Intellectual Property: While industrializing, China had very relaxed rules around intellectual property protection, which allowed Chinese businesses to experiment and innovate within the SEZs, including learning from foreign techniques. This allowed and incentivized companies to move up and down the value chain to more technologically sophisticated production, developing technological and management competencies to maximize quality (and minimize or mitigate environmental impact).

Finally, China's long-term industrial policy has successfully promoted industrial growth and development. On the other hand, African countries have been dependent on exporting raw materials and have not been successful in promoting industrialization.

In conclusion, while it may be tempting to view China as a model for African countries to follow, it is important to recognize the many differences between these two regions. African countries face unique challenges that cannot be easily overcome by simply copying China's experience. Instead, they should focus on developing their own unique strategies for industrial development that take into account the specific context and resources of their own countries. They would have to start by investing in education and infrastructure, promoting economic diversification, and implementing policies that support industrial growth and development.

6. The Important Lesson to Learn from Africa

Africa, the oldest and the second-largest continent in the world, is often overlooked and undervalued. However, there are many valuable lessons that the world can learn from this diverse and resilient continent.

6.1. LESSON FROM THE RESILIENCE AND DETERMINATION OF BLACK AFRICANS

The history of black Africans teaches us many important lessons about the world's future. Black Africans have endured many challenging historical experiences, including the transatlantic slave trade, colonialism, racism, and recent political and economic challenges. Despite these difficulties, they have survived and thrived, and their history is a powerful reminder of the human spirit's resilience, determination, and ingenuity.

One of the most important lessons that the history of black Africans teaches us about the world's future is the importance of resistance and resilience in facing adversity. Throughout history, black Africans have faced some of the most extreme forms of discrimination and oppression, yet they have been able to resist and overcome these obstacles. This resilience and determination are a testament to the strength of the human spirit and serve as a powerful example of what can be achieved when people refuse to give up in the face of difficulties. In the future, we must learn from the resilience of black Africans and be pre-pared to face and overcome the challenges that will arise.

Another important lesson that the history of black Africans teaches us about the future of the world is the importance of cultural heritage and tradition. Black Africans have been able to preserve their languages, music, dance, art, and other cultural expressions, which have played a key role in maintaining a sense of identity and community. Throughout history, black Africans have had to navigate the complex interplay between tradition and modernity, and they have been able to do so in a way that allows them to maintain their cultural identity while embracing new opportunities and ideas. This ability to balance tradition and modernity is a valuable lesson for the world, as it highlights the importance of preserving cultural heritage and tradition while being open to new ideas and ways of living. This cultural heritage is also a vital part of their identity and sense of self-worth, which helps them to maintain their resilience and determination in the face of adversity. For the future, it is essential to learn from the importance of preserving cultural heritage and tradition and how it can help communities maintain their identity.

The world can also learn from the sense of community and solidarity that exists among black Africans. Despite their many challenges, black Africans have always had strong communities, whether family, ethnic or religious, that have supported them. These communities have been instrumental in helping black Africans to overcome adversity and to build a better future for themselves and their families. The world can learn from this and understand the importance of building strong and supportive communities, which can play a vital role in helping people to overcome difficult situations and achieve their goals.

The history of black Africans also teaches us about the importance of challenging and resisting systems of oppression and discrimination. From the Civil Rights Movement in the United States to the anti-apartheid struggle in South Africa, black Africans have been at the forefront of efforts to combat discrimination and racism. They have also been instrumental in advocating for the rights of marginalized communities, such as women and the LGBTQ+ community. They have played a key role in raising awareness about poverty, hunger, and lack of access to education and healthcare. This history teaches us that it is essential to challenge and resist oppression and discrimination systems and fight for social and economic justice. In the future, it is important to continue this work to create a more just and equitable world for all.

Another important lesson is the importance of thinking creatively and finding new solutions to old problems. Throughout history, black Africans have had to find new ways to survive and thrive in the face of adversity, and they have been able to do so through their creativity and innovation. In the future, the world needs to learn from this history and be willing to think creatively and find new solutions to old problems. By doing so, we can be better equipped to address future challenges.

Lastly, it also teaches us about the importance of self-reliance and self-sufficiency. Throughout history, black Africans have had to rely on themselves and their communities to survive and thrive, and they have been able to do so through their self-reliance and self-sufficiency. This ability to rely on oneself and one's community is a valuable lesson for the world, as it highlights the importance of community support systems that teach and encourage independent self-reliance

In conclusion, the history of black Africans teaches us many important lessons about the world's future. We can learn from their resilience, determination, ingenuity, the importance of resistance, cultural heritage and tradition, challenging and re-sisting systems of oppression, adaptability, and innovation. By understanding these lessons, we can work towards creating a more just and equitable world for all.

6.2. LESSONS ABOUT CLIMATE CHANGE FROM A BLACK AFRICAN'S PERSPECTIVE

Climate change is a global issue that affects everyone, regard-less of race or ethnicity. However, the black African perspec-tive on climate change offers valuable insights that can help us better understand and address the issue. From their perspec-tive, we can learn important lessons about the intersection of environmental degradation, social inequality, and historical legacy.

One of the most important lessons that can be learned from the black African perspective is the impact of historical lega-cy on climate change. Throughout history, black Africans have been disproportionately affected by environmental degrada-tion and climate change, which can be attributed to the legacy of colonialism and exploitation. For example, during the colo-nial period, natural resources were extracted from the conti-nent without regard for their long-term sustainability, leading to deforestation and desertification. Furthermore, the legacy of slavery and forced labour has led to the overuse of land and the destruction of ecosystems. This historical legacy is still felt today, as black African communities are disproportionately af-fected by climate change and are more likely to live in areas vulnerable to its impacts.

Another important lesson that can be learned from the black African perspective is the importance of community-based approaches to addressing climate change. Throughout history, black Africans have relied on their communities for support and resources, and they have developed a deep understanding of the importance of community-based approaches to addressing environmental challenges. This understanding is particularly relevant today, as climate change is affecting communities around the globe. By learning from the community-based approach of black Africans, we can develop more effective strategies for addressing climate change based on community engagement and empowerment.

Additionally, from the black African perspective, we can learn about the importance of equity and social justice in addressing climate change. This understanding is particularly relevant today, as climate change affects marginalized communities more than others. By learning from the experiences of black Africans, we can develop more effective strategies for addressing climate change that is based on equity and social justice.

Another important lesson that can be learned from the black African perspective is the importance of traditional knowledge and practices in addressing climate change. By learning from the traditional knowledge and practices of black Africans, we can develop more effective strategies for addressing climate change that are based on a deep understanding of the natural world. For example, traditional farming practices that black Africans have used for centuries, such as crop rotation, intercropping, and agroforestry, have been more resilient to climate change's impacts than modern monoculture farming methods. These traditional practices not only help to increase crop yields but also help to conserve soil and water resources and reduce the risk of soil erosion.

Moreover, traditional knowledge and practices in water management, such as rainwater harvesting, community-managed irrigation systems, and traditional water storage systems, can also be useful in addressing the impacts of climate change. These traditional practices are not only more sustainable but also more resilient to the impacts of climate change than modern water management systems.

Additionally, traditional knowledge and practices in forest management, such as selective logging and rotational farming, are more sustainable and resilient than modern logging practices. These traditional practices not only help to conserve forest resources but also help to reduce the risk of soil erosion and landslides.

One of the most important lessons we can learn from the history of black Africans is the importance of understanding the interdependence between human activity and the natural world. This understanding is particularly relevant in today's world, where climate change is one of humanity's most pressing issues. By understanding the interdependence between human activity and the natural world, we can better understand the causes and effects of climate change and develop more effective strategies for addressing it.

In conclusion, the black African perspective on climate change offers valuable insights that can help us better understand and address the issue. From this perspective, we can learn important lessons about the importance of traditional knowledge and practices in addressing climate change. By incorporating these lessons, we can develop more effective strategies based on sustainability, resilience, and equity principles. Furthermore, valuing and promoting traditional knowledge and practices can create a more inclusive and equitable approach to climate change, benefiting not just black Africans but all people around the globe.

6.3. LESSONS FROM AFRICA ABOUT MANAGING PANDEMICS

As of the end of 2021, Africa accounted for only 4.1% of the 4.3 million deaths reported globally, despite the continent containing 12.5% of the global population. Africa's comparatively low mortality rate from COVID-19 significantly defy early predictions of a mass COVID-19 catastrophe and show that Africa has salient lessons to teach the rest of the world.

At the beginning of the COVID-19 pandemic, there were many predictions of doom and gloom for Africa. Experts feared that the continent's weak healthcare systems, high poverty rates, and lack of clean water and sanitation would be particularly vulnerable to the virus. These predictions led to concerns that Africa could face a devastating outbreak, with millions of deaths and widespread economic devastation.

However, as the pandemic has progressed, it has become clear that these dire predictions have not come to fruition. Despite initial fears, the number of confirmed COVID-19 cases and deaths in Africa has been relatively low compared to other regions. According to the World Mortality Dataset, the mass infection spread, high rates of severe disease, and excess mortality due to COVID-19 on the continent did not materialise.

This book believes that analysing factors that helped Africa experience low morbidity and mortality from COVID-19 is essential and is a valuable global public health lesson.

Early Government Measures and Messaging: Many African governments enacted early response measures to the pandemic. On 5 February 2020, even before a single case was reported in the continent, the Africa CDC established the Africa Taskforce for Coronavirus (AFCOR). On 22 April 2020, the World Health Organization (WHO) highlighted examples of how Africa was leading the global response. By 15 April 2020, 96% of the 50 African countries had in place at least five 'stringent public health and social measures' to prepare for the emerging pandemic. Early border closures and lockdowns were enforced, resulting in less international connectivity to prevent viral importation from international flight arrivals. All these had an important early impact on slowing the spread.

African governments were able to implement this quickly because destructive epidemics are not a new phenomenon in Africa. The continent is constantly dealing with abundant infectious diseases (e.g., malaria, yellow fever, tuberculosis, Ebola, polio). Due to their familiarity with these epidemics, many governments have developed effective public health programs with messaging to unify the community and highlight the need for preventative action among individuals. Unlike the government mistrust in the western world, African population is better prepared to adhere to government public health recommendations.

Population Distribution and Structure of Social Networks: Population structure and spatial distribution strongly predict the patterns of SARS-CoV-2 transmission in communities. Africa is the least urbanised global region, with 55% of the continent's population living in rural areas with wide variations across countries. In addition, few of the older African population live in nursing homes, unlike the US, where one-third to one-half of deaths occurred in elderly nursing homes.

A Largely Outdoor Existence: Infected persons usually transmit the virus through coughing, sneezing, talking, singing, and breathing, meaning that living environments matter. Studies show that coronavirus transmission is concentrated in indoor settings, up to 19 times more than outdoors. As a result, built environments in urban areas which require ventilation, air-conditioning/heating, wastewater, and sewer systems have been shown to increase the spread of the virus. Whereas rural homes that are well-ventilated with outside air significantly reduce the chance of viral transmission compared to tightly enclosed indoor spaces in developed countries. In addition, African livelihoods in the rural area largely depend on agriculture and pastoralism favours dawn-to-dusk outdoor lifestyles. Prolonged, year-round outdoor living with direct exposure to sun and UV light in mostly warm and tropical climates also partially reduced transmission,with the additional benefit of vitamin D produced by the sun.

Demographic Pyramid: It is well documented that the COVID-19 burden is heavily skewed towards older populations. Compared with the demographic group of 5–17 years, the demographic of 65–74 years is 35 times more likely to become hospitalised and 1100 times more likely to die from COVID-19. Africa has the youngest population among all global regions, with a median age of 19.7 years

Pre-Existing Conditions: It is well known that people with pre-existing conditions, such as diabetes, chronic respiratory diseases, obesity, and hypertension, have a greatly increased risk of moderate to severe complications from COVID-19 infection. These conditions are considerably less prevalent in low-income, and lower-middle-income countries (LICs and LMICs) compared to higher-income countries (HICs). The majority of the health burden in African countries comes from infectious diseases.

Trained Immunity: The phenomenon of trained immunity may be tempering the COVID-19 statistics in Africa. For example, live vaccines activate innate immune systems, protecting against future infections from other pathogens. Recent data suggest regions with mandated BCG vaccinations have lower COVID-19 disease burden.

The "Hygiene Hypothesis": Is the hypothesis that some environments advantage populations against certain forms of infection and disease due to chronic exposure to a multi-microbial environment, potentially producing protective immune effects when encountering new pathogens. There has been some concern regarding regions that use ultra-hygienic practices, exemplified by the overuse of hand sanitiser and other disinfection practices in many countries. Given that 22 of the 25 most vulnerable countries to infectious disease epidemics are in Africa, the continent carries the heaviest burden of infectious diseases. Infection by malaria alone may overstimulate the immune system and confer an immune advantage when compared to nonexposed populations.

The Historical use of Natural Medicine for Primary Care: Natural medicine use in Africa triggered a WHO-AFRO expert panel in September 2020 to endorse a protocol for the clinical investigation of herbal medicine for COVID-19.

Traditional medicine is a healing method with its own concept of health and disease. It comprises unscientific knowledge systems that have developed over generations within various societies before the era of western medicine. Knowledge is passed on orally from father to son through generations and is jealously guarded in certain families. The components of traditional medicine encompass herbal medicine, therapeutic fasting and dieting, and more. The practitioners include herbalists, diviners and midwives.

Many traditional medicine practitioners in Africa are people without formal education who have received knowledge of medicinal plants and their effects on the human body from their forebears [Bodeker et al., 1994]. They have a deep and personal involvement in the healing process and protect the therapeutic knowledge by keeping it secret.

While modern pharmaceuticals and medical procedures remain unaffordable and inaccessible to many African people due to their relatively high cost and concentration of health centres in urban centres, conversely, traditional medicine is affordable to ordinary Africans in rural and urban areas.

This natural, holistic care has been influential for thousands of years and has remained to this day. The remedies made from indigenous plants play a crucial role in the health of millions of Africans. One estimate puts the number of Africans who routinely use traditional medicine services as their first choice before western medicine to be as high as 85 per cent in Sub-Saharan Africa. For example, in Ghana, traditional medicine caters to about 75-85 per cent of rural people and 45-65 per cent of urban dwellers. Regarding accessibility, there is one traditional health practitioner for every 200-400 Ugandans compared to one western-trained doctor per 20,000. These statistics show that the continued popularity of these treatments is not likely to not decline in the near future.

China, India, Nigeria, the US, and the WHO have all made moderate research investments in traditional herbal medicines.

For traditional medicine to respond to the challenge of science and to be accepted by all, there has to be some serious input of funds to undertake in-depth research into its efficacy, safety, quality, standardisation and regulation.

Genetics: Some genetic, and immunological factors could be playing a role in shielding Africa from the brunt of the pandemic. Studies have shown that African populations have an exceptionally high proportion of O-positivity at nearly 50%, which is higher than in White and Asian populations. It is possible that this increased O prevalence could confer a greater protective effect in African populations compared with other groups with less O prevalence.

Broader Sociocultural Implications:. One study of the top 50 countries with the highest cases suggests that increased income inequality was associated with increased severe cases and mortality. Across the US, Brazil, South Africa, and Europe increased mortality has been reported among minority groups such as Africans and Asians. In contrast, in many African cities, the social and political elites are the ones who can afford to live and work in airconditioned closed spaces, increasing susceptibility to infection through close, indoor contact with others

Relatively low severity and death due to COVID-19 in Africa present somewhat of a paradox. Despite early 'doomsday' predictions for Africa, the continent succeeded in stemming the first wave of SARS-CoV-2 spread. On the whole, the factors discussed here have contributed to modulating disease spread and severity; however, the strength of evidence of each varies.

Alongside facing the lowest quality of health systems,

6.4. LESSON FROM AFRICA THE TRUTH AND RECONCILIATION COMMISSION

The Truth and Reconciliation Commission (TRC) was a South African body established to investigate human rights violations that occurred during the apartheid era. The TRC's main goal was to provide a platform for victims to share their stories and to promote reconciliation between different racial and ethnic groups in the country. The commission's work was ground-breaking and provided important lessons for other countries dealing with similar issues.

One of the main lessons that can be learned from the TRC is the importance of addressing past injustices. The commission's work helped to acknowledge and confront the atrocities committed during the apartheid era, which was essential for the healing process of both victims and perpetrators. This process of acknowledging and facing up to past wrongs is crucial for any society that wants to move forward in a healthy and just way.

Another important lesson is the power of forgiveness and reconciliation. The TRC's focus on promoting reconciliation between different groups in South Africa was a key factor in the country's peaceful transition to a democratic government. The commission's work helped to create a space for dialogue and understanding between different groups, which was crucial for building a more inclusive and harmonious society.

The TRC's work also highlighted the importance of providing reparations and support to victims of human rights violations. The commission's recommendations for reparations, such as financial compensation and psychological support, helped provide justice for victims and their families. This aspect of the TRC's work is an important reminder that any society that wants to move forward from past injustices must also provide support and assistance to those affected by them.

Additionally, the TRC also demonstrated the power of storytelling and testimony in the process of healing and reconciliation. By providing a platform for victims to share their stories, the commission helped to give voice to those who had been silenced and marginalized during the apartheid era. This act of listening and bearing witness to the experiences of victims was crucial in creating a sense of empathy and understanding among different groups in the country

Another important lesson from the TRC is the need for a comprehensive and inclusive reconciliation process. The commission's work was inclusive of different racial and ethnic groups, as well as different genders and sexual orientations. This inclusivity was important in addressing the complex and intersecting forms of oppression during the apartheid era. It also serves as a reminder that any reconciliation process must be inclusive and consider how different groups may have been affected by past injustices.

Furthermore, the TRC also showed that the reconciliation process is ongoing and requires ongoing commitment. The commission's work was only a first step in the long process of healing and reconciliation in South Africa. There is still much work to be done to address the structural inequalities in the country and promote reconciliation and understanding between different groups.

In conclusion, the Truth and Reconciliation Commission of South Africa provided many valuable lessons for societies dealing with past injustices. It highlighted the importance of acknowledging and addressing past wrongs, promoting reconciliation, and providing reparations and support to victims. Additionally, the commission's work demonstrated the power of storytelling and testimony, the need for a comprehensive and inclusive process of reconciliation, and the ongoing nature of the process of reconciliation. These lessons are essential for any society that wants to move forward from past injustices and create a more just and peaceful society.

6.5. OTHER IMPORTANT LESSONS FROM AFRICA THAT THE WORLD SHOULD NOT DISCARD

Africa, the second-largest continent in the world, is a diverse and complex region with a rich history and culture. The continent has faced numerous challenges throughout its history, from colonialism and imperialism to poverty and political instability. However, despite these challenges, Africa has much to teach the rest of the world.

1. We Need Much Less than we Have: African people are the most joyful people on Earth, yet they have access to a fraction of what most Europeans and Americans take for granted. The phrase "we need much less than we have" refers to the idea that, as a society, we often have more than we need to live a fulfilling and happy life. This can be seen in various aspects of our lives, including material possessions, consumption, and even information.

This African belief is reflected in the way of life of many African communities, which are characterized by simplicity, self-sufficiency, and a deep connection to the natural world. One of the key reasons for this belief is that many African societies have lived in close harmony with nature for centuries. This way of life has led to an understanding that the natural world is a source of sustenance and that the earth's resources must be used responsibly and sustainably. Traditional African practices reflect this understanding through principles of communal land ownership and collective decision-making based on cooperation and mutual aid principles.

Water is a Limited Resource: Water is a vital resource for all life on Earth, yet it is also a limited resource that should be used wisely and sparingly. Many African communities have long struggled with water scarcity due to drought, desertification, or inadequate infrastructure. This has led to a deep understanding of the importance of water conservation and the need to use water resources responsibly. These beliefs are implemented through traditional practices such as rainwater harvesting, community-managed irrigation systems, and traditional water storage systems based on water conservation and management principles.

Complete Silence Feeds the Soul: The African bush, with its wide-open spaces, towering trees, and diverse wildlife, is a place of tranquillity and serenity that can feed the soul. The African belief that complete silence feeds the soul is rooted in the deep connection that many African societies have with nature and the spiritual significance of the natural world. This has led to an understanding that the natural world is not only a source of sustenance but also a source of wisdom and spiritual nourishment. Meditation, prayer, and rituals, which are often performed in natural settings, are based on the principles of connecting with the natural world.

Homelessness is Unnecessary: Many African societies believe that homelessness is unnecessary and everyone has the right to a safe and secure home. This belief is rooted in community and collective responsibility values deeply ingrained in many African cultures. The concept of "home" is not limited to physical structures but also encompasses a sense of belonging and community connection. "Ubuntu" is the belief in a universal bond of sharing that connects all humanity. This belief emphasizes the importance of community, that everyone is responsible for the well-being of others, and that access to a safe and secure home is essential for physical and emotional well-being.

Wildlife and Wild Places Enrich our Spirit in Irreplaceable Ways: Africa is home to some of the most diverse and spectacular wildlife on the planet, and it is no surprise that the continent's people believe that wildlife and wild places enrich their spirit. For many Africans, the natural world is not just a resource to be exploited but a sacred and integral part of their culture, identity, and way of life. It's important to appreciate and protect the wildlife and wild places in Africa as they are not only a source of inspiration, guidance, and spiritual nourishment but also play an essential role in the continent's economy and livelihoods and educating and inspiring future generations.

Almost Anything can be Recycled or Reused: Many African societies have a long-standing tradition of resourcefulness and recycling. This belief is rooted in the understanding that resources are scarce and must be used efficiently and effectively. This belief is reflected in how many African communities use waste materials. They deeply understand how to use waste materials to create new products, such as turning plastic bags into mats and sandals, old clothes into new clothes, or old tires into new products. They also have found ways to use agricultural waste to create new products, such as turning agricultural waste into fertilizer or using it to feed livestock. We can create a more sustainable, resilient, and equitable world for all by valuing and promoting this belief.

Creativity is Innate and Shows up in the Least Expected Situations: In many African cultures, creativity is seen as an individual endeavour rather than a communal one. For example, in traditional African drumming, the lead drummer is not the only creative force; the entire ensemble is expected to improvise and bring new ideas to the music. This belief is rooted in the idea that creativity is not something that can be taught or learned but is a natural part of human nature. African cultures value and celebrate creativity in various forms as a fundamental aspect of human existence.

Anything Can and Should be Celebrated: Many African cultures believe anything can and should be celebrated. That the belief that life is precious means every moment should be cherished and appreciated. African culture encourages dance and song to celebrate life anytime, anywhere, at any time. Africans dance and sing when they plant rice, harvest rice, and then again when eating it. They dance and sing for weddings, births, engagements, deaths, for someone leaving, and someone coming. It's an admirable and wonderful custom. Furthermore, African cultures also believe that everyday moments should be celebrated and the celebration of life should be inclusive and involve the entire community.

There is Always Time: Africans believe that time is not a fixed and finite resource but can be stretched and expanded to accommodate the present moment's needs. No one should be in a rush. "I have to go," are four words that are overused in the American language. Getting to the next 'thing' we have to do becomes habitual. Are all the things we must fit into our lives necessary? Many African cultures believe that there is always time. Time is a fluid concept that can be shaped and moulded according to the situation's needs. Time should be used wisely and not wasted, shared and not hoarded. Time should be spent on living in the present moment, enjoying and appreciating the little things in life, hard work, productivity, and building and strengthening relationships with others.

The Word 'Alone' Doesn't Exist in Most African Tribal Languages: Americans are an isolated and isolating culture. We live far from our families, hardly know our neighbours, and keep so busy we don't have quality time for friends and family. In many African cultures, the concept of "aloneness" or alone does not exist. Being alone means being disconnected from the community and is, therefore, not a part of the cultural lexicon. The belief in "Ubuntu" further strengthens the notion of being part of a collective and not alone.

Gratefulness is a Powerful State of Mind: In her latest book, Christine Carter writes, "the happiest people are also the most grateful". Africans are the most grateful people. Many African cultures believe gratefulness is a powerful state of mind and a fundamental aspect of human existence, reflected in the many traditional rituals and ceremonies used to express gratitude. Gratitude has a positive impact on one's mental and physical well-being and can also have a positive impact on one's relationships and the community.

Emphasis on Hospitality:

This belief is rooted in the idea that showing hospitality and generosity towards others is a moral duty and an important aspect of community building and social cohesion. Many African cultures believe that hospitality is an essential aspect of human existence. It's about providing tangible goods, emotional support, and a sense of belonging. It is also a way of showing respect and honour to guests and building trust and goodwill. The traditional African concept of "Karibu", meaning "welcome", expresses hospitality and generosity towards guests. Many African cultures strongly emphasise welcoming guests with open arms and providing them with food, shelter and other necessities.

6.6. THE POTENTIAL OF INTRA-AFRICAN TRADE

Intra-African trade refers to the trade of goods and services between African countries. Despite being a continent with a large and diverse population and rich natural resources, Africa has a relatively low level of intra-African trade compared to another internal trading in other regions. However, there is a growing recognition of the potential benefits of increasing intra-African trade for economic growth and development.

One of the main benefits of intra-African trade is the potential to reduce dependence on exports to developed markets. Africa has been facing significant trade barriers in developed markets, such as high tariffs and non-tariff measures, which make it difficult for African countries to export their products. By increasing intra-African trade, African countries can diversify their export markets and reduce their dependence on a few developed countries.

Africa's farmers can potentially grow enough food to feed the continent and avert future food crises if countries remove cross-border restrictions on food trade within the region. Africa would also generate an extra US$20 billion in yearly earnings if African leaders can agree to dismantle trade barriers that blunt more regional dynamism.

The new report suggests that if the continent's leaders can embrace more dynamic inter-regional trade, Africa's farmers, the majority of whom are women, could meet the continent's rising demand and benefit from a major growth opportunity. It would also create more jobs in services such as distribution while reducing poverty and cutting back on expensive food imports. Africa's production of staple foods is worth at least US$50 billion a year.

Unfortunately, only five per cent of all cereals imported by African countries come from other African countries. At the same time, huge tracts of fertile land, around 400 million hectares, remain uncultivated, and yields remain a fraction of those obtained by farmers elsewhere in the world.

Another benefit of intra-African trade is the potential to create jobs and economic opportunities. Intra-African trade can help to create jobs and economic opportunities by increasing demand for goods and services within the continent and by increasing the volume of trade between African countries. This could help stimulate economic growth and development and improve the population's standard of living.

In addition, by increasing trade between African countries, intra-African trade can help promote regional integration and cooperation, encourage the development of regional value chains and infrastructure, and foster regional trade agreements.

However, several challenges must be addressed to increase intra-African trade.

Lack of Infrastructure and Connectivity within the Continent: One of the main factors hindering intra-African trade is the lack of infrastructure and connectivity. Africa has a relatively low level of connective infrastructure compared to other regions of the world, which makes it difficult for African countries to trade with each other. Poor transportation infrastructure, limited access to electricity, and inadequate telecommunications networks make it difficult for goods and services to move between countries.

Lack of Trade Agreements and Policies that Support intra-African Trade: Africa has relatively few trade agreements and policies that support intra-African trade compared to other regions of the world. Lack of harmonized trade policies, tariffs and non-tariff barriers to trade, and lack of a common currency, make it difficult for African countries to trade with each other.

Non-Tariff Barriers to Trade: Non-tariff barriers to trade, such as bureaucracy, lack of standardization, and lack of transparency, also hinder intra-African trade. These barriers create delays and increase trade costs, making it difficult for trade between countries.

Lack of Access to Finance and Technology: Many African countries and businesses have limited access to finance and technology, which makes it difficult for them to compete in global markets and with each other.

Political Instability and Conflicts in some Countries: Political conflict also hinders intra-African trade. Conflicts and political instability disrupt trade and make it difficult for businesses to operate and for goods and services to move between countries.

Therefore, to increase intra-African trade, these challenges must be addressed. With the implementation of trade policies and investments in infrastructure, Africa can increase its intra-African trade and create jobs and economic opportunities for its population.

6.7. THE WORLD SHOULD STOP PLUNDERING AFRICA'S WEALTH

Research has shown that financial flows outweigh aid and loans to the African continent to tax havens and the costs of climate change mitigation. According to the African Union, illicit financial flows account for $68 billion a year. African countries received $162 billion in 2015, mainly in loans, aid and personal remittances. But in the same year, $203 billion was taken from the continent, either directly through multinationals repatriating profits and illegally moving money into tax havens or by costs imposed by the rest of the world through climate change adaptation and mitigation. This meant that more

THE IMPORTANT LESSON TO LEARN FROM AFRICA ❏ 137

wealth leaves Africa every year than enters it — by more than $40 billion from the 47 African countries where many people remain impoverished.

The prevailing media narrative in western society is that Africa is poor and needs western help is a distraction and misleading. What African countries need is for the rest of the world to stop systematically looting them. While the form of colonial plunder may have changed over time, its fundamental nature remains unchanged.

Africa has considerable riches; for example, South Africa's potential mineral wealth is estimated to be around $2.5 trillion, while the mineral reserves of the Democratic Republic of the Congo are estimated to be worth $24 trillion. However, foreign private corporations continue to own and exploit the continent's natural resources.

Economic development is a lost cause in Africa while the western world is haemorrhaging billions yearly to extractive industries, western tax havens and illegal logging and fishing. Some serious structural changes need to be made to promote economic policies that enable African countries to best serve the needs of their people rather than simply being cash cows for western corporations and governments.

There are 1.2 billion people in Africa, and the $41 billion loss every year will put the overall GDP of Africa at some $7.7 trillion since the continent became independent 80 years ago. The release of this money would enable African people to invest and learn, adapt technologies and access markets.

 Dr Jason Hickel, an economic anthropologist, explains, "One of the many problems with the aid narrative is it leads the public to believe that rich countries are helping developing countries, but that narrative skews the often extractive relationship that exists between rich and poor countries. The western world has a direct responsibility to fix the problem if they want to claim to care about international poverty at all". They can do this by preventing companies with subsidiaries based in tax havens from operations in African countries, transforming aid into a process that genuinely benefits the continent, and re-configuring aid from a system of voluntary donations to one of repatriation for damage caused.

International corruption watchdog stated that high street banks in the United Kingdom had helped fuel corruption in Nigeria by accepting millions of dollars in deposits from dubious politicians in the West African nation. Global Witness found that five leading banks have failed to adequately investigate the source of tens of millions of dollars taken from two Nigerian governors accused of corruption.

Like other banks, UK Banks are quick to penalise ordinary customers for minor infractions but seem less concerned about the large sums of dirty money passing through their accounts. Large-scale corruption is impossible without a bank willing to process payments from dodgy sources or hold accounts for corrupt politicians.

Global Witness acknowledged that Barclays, NatWest, Royal Bank of Scotland (RBS), HSBC, and Switzerland's UBS were laundering through British banks. Yet, no British bank has been publicly fined for taking corrupt funds, whether willingly or through negligence.

The World Bank and the International Monetary Fund (IMF) were set up during the end of the Second World War to rebuild the economies of Europe. They, too, were an accomplice to the underdevelopment in Africa. The World Bank and the IMF implemented their policies by offering loans to developing countries, but only if the developing countries privatized their economies and allowed western corporations free access to their raw materials and markets. This was a poverty trap, and many developing countries realized it when it was too late.

That was the beginning of many of the problems we face in Africa today. We are in a vicious cycle of poverty, and there seems to be no way out. Western corporations flourish while the poor in Africa and other parts of the developing world continue to die in poverty.

The public's general perception is that the World Bank, the IMF and the World Trade Organization (WTO) help fight poverty and hunger in the developing world. However, in reality, this is far from the truth. It is a new form of warfare whereby the rich western corporations employ deception, the poverty of the poor, and the ignorance of the innocent as top weapons of mass destruction. The World Bank, the IMF and the WTO are the triple enemies of progress in almost every developing country today. Here are examples of how the World Bank, the IMF and the WTO operate in Sub-Saharan Africa.

Take a country like Ghana, for example. Ghana is blessed with an abundance of natural resources. The World Bank and the IMF are very interested in countries such as Ghana, where they can easily control natural resources and markets.

There used to be some prosperous rice farming communities in the northern parts of Ghana. Ghana's government gave those rice-producing farmers farming subsidies to produce rice on a larger scale to help feed the nation. However, the WTO, the World Bank and the IMF stood in and told the Ghanaian government that they would not give Ghana any more loans unless it cut the farming subsidies. The main reason was that Ghana had to import rice from "partner" western countries such as the United States (a major partner of the World Bank and the IMF).

Now Ghana imports most of its rice from abroad at huge prices yearly. So at the end of the day, Ghana owes the World Bank and the IMF huge amounts of money. However, the money did not remain in the Ghanaian economy because Ghana had to use the loan to import food from abroad. Meanwhile, the rice-producing communities in Ghana could have helped produce enough rice to feed the nation (and even exported some abroad to make more profit). Now, the northern communities in Ghana remain the poorest in the country, with no access to better jobs or opportunities. Young boys and girls, some as young as 9, are migrating to the southern parts of the country to major cities and towns such as Kumasi and Accra (a perilous journey for kids),in search of jobs so they can take care of their poor dying families back home. Most of these kids, locally known as "kayayo", never return home.

That is why most developing countries owe the World Bank and the IMF large loans. 'Debt cancellations' by these institutions does not mean they forgive developing countries' debts. The World Bank and the IMF never forgive, and because of the huge debts developing countries owe, they (the World Bank, the IMF, the WTO, etc.) control almost all the affairs of those developing countries. In other words, if you don't obey what the World Bank (or the IMF, etc.) say, you must pay back the debt, and because you cannot pay back the debt, you must obey whatever they tell you to do.

7. Conclusion

Throughout this book, we have examined the historical portrayal of Africa as a "basket case" and the emerging narrative of Africa as a "breadbasket" for the world. We have explored the negative consequences of the "basket case" narrative on the continent's economic and social development and how the "breadbasket" narrative has the potential to reshape the global perception of Africa.

The growth of Africa's middle class, the expansion of its industries, and the potential for the continent to take a more active role in shaping its own economic and social development are all indicators of Africa's emergence as a "breadbasket." However, it is important to recognize that the "breadbasket" narrative is not without its challenges and that any narrative of Africa's potential for economic growth and development must be based on a realistic and nuanced understanding of the continent's challenges and opportunities.

One of the key challenges for Africa in becoming a "breadbasket" is the need for sustained economic growth. This will require addressing the root causes of poverty and inequality, such as poor governance, lack of access to education and healthcare, and inadequate infrastructure. Additionally, the continent must address political instability, corruption, and conflict, which can undermine economic growth and development.

Another challenge is the need to diversify Africa's economies to reduce the continent's dependence on commodity exports, which are subject to volatile global prices. Developing the continent's domestic markets and value chains, as well as investing in manufacturing and services industries, will be key in achieving this goal.

Despite these challenges, there are many reasons to be optimistic about Africa's potential as a "breadbasket" for the world. The continent's abundant natural resources, young and rapidly growing population, and increasing participation in the global economy all point to a bright future. Additionally, Africa has a rich cultural heritage and a vibrant civil society, which can play a key role in driving economic and social development.

There are also many valuable lessons that the world can learn from this diverse and resilient continent. Africa is the oldest and the second-largest continent in the world. One of the most important lessons that the history of black Africans teaches us about the world's future is the importance of resistance and resilience in facing adversity. This resilience and determination are a testament to the strength of the human spirit and serve as a powerful example of what can be achieved when people refuse to give up in the face of difficulties.

In conclusion, Africa has enormous potential to be a breadbasket for the world. Still, that potential can only be realised if the continent is supported in addressing its economic and social challenges. Only then can Africa truly become a breadbasket for the world and be able to shape its own economic and social development. This book aims to provide a more nuanced understanding of the continent's challenges and opportunities to contribute to the ongoing dialogue of Africa's potential.

GLOSSARY AND TERMS

Algorithm — An established, detailed, structured step-by-step instruction to solve a problem or carry out a task.

Apartheid — A policy of racial segregation practised in South Africa.

Arabs — A people group from the Middle East who invaded and conquered North Africa in the 700s CE.

Berber — The native peoples of North Africa.

Caravan — A group of traders typically travelling across the desert using camels.

Cassava — A herb-like tropical plant with a long stalk, mostly found underwater, that yields a nutritious starch

Cholera — A disease marked by severe vomiting and dysentery that is often fatal.

Caste — A group or division of people that defines social order and rank.

Christianity- A religion based on the teachings of Jesus Christ and the belief that he was the son of Go.d

Civilization — The culture and way of life of a people, nation or period regarded as a stage in the development of organized society.

Climate — The average weather conditions of a place; a prevailing environment.

Colony — A region or state established as the possession of a separate nation.

Continent — A large continuous expanse of land. Africa is one of the Earth's continents.

Deforestation — The state of having been cleared of forests.

Desertification — The process of becoming desert, either from inappropriate land management or climate change.

Developed country — A country with a highly organized economy.

Dialect — A regional variety of a language.

Drought — An extended and stressful spell of dry weather in a region.

Earthquakes — A shaking or trembling of a portion of the earth.

Economic — Related to the production, distribution and consumption of goods and services.

Ecosystem — An ecological community together with its environment, functioning as a unit.

Endangered — A plant or animal threatened with extinction.

Ethnic — Of, or relating to, a sizable group of people sharing a common and distinctive racial, national, religious, linguistic, or cultural heritage.

Evolution — A gradual process in which something changes into a different and usually more complex or better form.

Famine — An extreme scarcity of food.

The founder effect — The loss of genetic variation that occurs when a new population is established by a very small number of individuals from a larger population.

Generation — A single stage in a family, clan or tribes history. Children, parents and grandparents represent three generations.

Grassland — Land covered with long grass and low-growing herbs.

Griot — A storyteller, musician, and historian in West Africa.

Hieroglyphics — A system of writing used by the Egyptians that used symbols and pictures.

HIV/AIDS — Human Immunodeficiency Virus / Acquired Immunodeficiency Syndrome.

Islam — A religion that believes in Allah and the teaching of the prophet Muhammad. It spread to North Africa in the 700sCE.

Ivory — A hard, white material formed from the tusks of animals such as elephants. It was used to make jewellery and other ornaments.

Kingdom — A country, city, or state whose head-of-state is a king or queen.

Koran — The sacred book of Islam wherein the revelations of Allah are given to Muhammad.

Malnutrition — Poor nutrition because of an insufficient or poorly balanced diet or faulty digestion or utilization of foods.

Mediterranean — Relates to the body of water that separates Africa, Europe and Asia, or to the land and people around it.

Migrant — One who moves from one country to another or any person who moves for access to work, food or climate.

Muslim — A person who follows the religion of Islam.

Nomadic — A group of people who have no fixed residence but move from place to place.

Nutrition — The processes by which a person takes in and utilizes food material to maintain health.

Nomads — People that travel from place to place to find food and pasture for their livestock.

Population — The number of people in a designated area.

Post-colonial — Of, relating to, or being the time following the establishment of independence in a colony.

Pyramid — A monumental structure with four sides that meet at a point at the top. The Egyptians and the Kushites built pyramids generally as tombs for their pharaohs.

Rainforest — A dense forest found in areas of heavy rainfall. Some of central and western Africa is rainforest.

Sahara Desert — Large desert in North Africa between the Mediterranean Sea and Central/West Africa.

Savanna — Grassland containing scattered trees.

Slave trade — The capturing, transporting, buying, and selling of people as slaves.

Slave — A person held as property.

Swahili — An ethnic group in East Africa; the language spoken by many East African nations including Kenya and Uganda.

Tribe — A group of families, clans, or generations.

Tsetse Fly — Any of several sub-Saharan flies including those that transmit diseases, such as sleeping sickness, a serious illness marked by fever, lethargy, tremors, and weight loss.

Urban — Relating to, or characteristics of, a city.

Volcanic eruption — The explosion at an opening in the earth's crust marked by molten rock and steam, usually appearing like a mountain from the rock and ash produced.

Reference

African arms imports increased 45 per cent over last decade — SIPRI. Written by defenceWeb, 18th Mar 2015. Retrieved 16/03/19. *https://www.defenceweb.co.za/industry/industry-industry/african-arms-imports-increased-45-per-cent-over-last-decade-sipri/*

Ann Gibbons, (2017), "New Gene Variants Reveal The Evolution Of Human Skin Colour". *Www.sciencemag.com*. retrieved Feb 28, 2022.)

Browne, B. (2011). Africa and the World. The Nations Newspaper, February 10, p.7.

Calderon, Cesar; Kambou, Gerard; Korman, Vijdan; Kubota, Megumi; Cantu Canales, Catalina. 2019. *Africa's Pulse, No. 19, April 2019 : An Analysis of Issues Shaping Africa's Economic Future*. Washington, DC: World Bank. © World Bank. https://openknowledge.worldbank.org/handle/10986/31499 License: CC BY 3.0 IGO."

Economy of Africa. (2023, January 20). In Wikipedia. *https://en.wikipedia.org/wiki/Economy_of_Africa*

Founder effect. (2022, September 5). In Wikipedia. *https://en.wikipedia.org/wiki/Founder_effect*

Fadhlaoui-Zid K, Haber M, Martínez-Cruz B, Zalloua P, Benammar Elgaaied A, Comas D (2013-11-27).

Harley, George (1941). "Native African medicine with special reference to its practice in the Mano tribe of Liberia". Cambridge, Mass: Harvard University Press. p. 26. ISBN 978-0-674-18304-9. OCLC 598805544.

Jideofor Patrick Adibe (2009), "Who is an African? Identity, Citizenship and the Making of the Africa-Nation", Adonis & Abbey Publishers

List of World Heritage Sites in Africa. (2022, November 14). In Wikipedia. *https://en.wikipedia.org/wiki/List_of_World_Heritage_Sites_in_Africa*

Louissa Brooke-Holland. An Introduction To UK's Arms Export. House of Commons Library; Briefing Paper, No 8312, 16th May, 2018. *https://researchbriefings.files.parliament.uk/documents/CBP-8425/CBP08312.pdf*

Mineral industry of Africa. (2023, January 1). In Wikipedia. *https://en.wikipedia.org/wiki/Mineral_industry_of_Africa*

SIPRI Yearbook, 2015. Armament, Disarmament and International Security. Published in print and online in 2015 by Oxford University Press on behalf of Stockholm International Peace Research Institute. **ISSN:** 0953–0282, **ISBN:** 978-0-19-873781-0. *https://www.sipri.org/yearbook/2015/10*

Rethinking the Foundations of Export Diversification in Africa: THE CATALYTIC ROLE OF BUSINESS AND FINANCIAL SERVICES (2022).

TRADE AND DEVELOPMENT REPORT 2022 Development prospects in a fractured world: Global disorder and regional responses [Film].

Thomas R. Yager, Omayra Bermúdez-Lugo, Philip M. Mobbs, Harold R. Newman, Mowafa Taib, Glenn J. Wallace, and David R. Wilburn (August 2012). "The Mineral Industries of Africa"

UNITED NATIONS CONFERENCE ON TRADE AND DEVELOPMENT (2022)

Woods, Michael, 2009 *"Seven wonders of Ancient Africa"*, p. 61. Lerner books,United Kingdom 2009. ISBN-10: 082257571X

"Zeufack, Albert G.; Calderon, Cesar; Kabundi, Alain; Kubota, Megumi; Korman, Vijdan; Raju, Dhushyanth; Abreha, Kaleb Girma; Kassa, Woubet; Owusu, Solomon. 2022. Africa's Pulse, No. 25, April 2022. Africa's Pulse;25. Washington, DC: World Bank. © World Bank. *https://openknowledge.worldbank.org/handle/10986/37281* License: CC BY 3.0 IGO."

https://www.theguardian.com/global-development-professionals-network/2017/jan/14/aid-in-reverse-how-poor-countries-develop-rich-countries

https://gfintegrity.org/press-release/new-report-on-unrecorded-capital-flight-finds-developing-countries-are-net-creditors-to-the-rest-of-the-world/

https://www.uneca.org/publications/illicit-financial-flows

https://www.businessinsider.co.za/fincen-files-south-africa-2020-9

http://www.madeinafricainitiative.com/

https://www.theguardian.com/global-development/2018/dec/21/one-third-of-uk-arms-sales-go-to-states-on-human-rights-watchlist-say-analysts https://www.theguardian.com/global-development/dat-ablog/2015/mar/20/africa-arms-imports-algeria-morocco-glob-al-weapons-trade

https://www.ft.com/content/4686e022-f58b-11e9-b018-3ef-8794b17c6

https://en.wikipedia.org/wiki/Economy_of_Africa